Activities for Preschool and Kindergarten Children

GROWING & LEARNING
THROUGH PLAY

by Charles H. Wolfgang,

Bea Mackender and

Mary E. Wolfgang

A PARENT/CAREGIVER BOOK

 **Judy/Instructo**™

Copyright © 1981 by Judy/Instructo. All rights reserved. Printed
in the United States of America. Except as permitted under the
Copyright Act of 1976, no part of this publication may be produced
or distributed in any form or by any means, or stored in a data base
or retrieval system, without the prior written permission
of the publisher.

Library of Congress Cataloging in Publication Data

Wolfgang, Charles H.
    Growing & learning through play.

    "A Parent/caregiver book."
    Bibliography: p. 142.
    Includes index.
    1. Creative activities and seat work—Handbooks,
manuals, etc.   2. Play—Handbooks, manuals, etc.
I. Mackender, Bea.   II. Wolfgang, Mary E.
III. Title.   IV. Title: Growing and learning through play.
LB1140.35.C74W64   372.5   81-5013
ISBN 0-382-29653-2   AACR2

Printed in the United States of America

10 9 8 7

AC
I58
G76
1981
Pre-K

Editor: Maureen H. Cook
Cover Design and Illustrations: Pat Traub
Page Layout: Ellie Pfautz
Typesetting: Rosanne McFadden

Editorial Consultant: Martha Hochschwender

Following the current convention in early childhood literature and for ease of reading, we are using the masculine pronoun when referring to the child throughout this book. We trust that you, the reader, will in your own mind, apply the feminine pronoun.

The Authors

5464

BELMONT COLLEGE LIBRARY
CURRICULUM LAB

Dedication

For our children
Lisa, Justin and Ellen Louise

contents

Why Play for Young Children?

In our work-oriented society, play often has a negative meaning.

> "Quit playing around."

> "You're wasting your time playing."

> "Playboy."

These are all expressions that show our lack of respect for play. But if we look closely, we will find that play is the central activity of young children. It is play that enables children to grow socially, emotionally, intellectually, and physically to their maxium potential.

The Value of Play for Social Development

The young child is not born with the ability to "get along" with others or to cooperate in activities of give and take. This skill of "learning to live and work with others" begins first as *isolated play*, exploring the parents' faces and bodies with their own body, and exploring and manipulating toys and objects (ages 0-2½). This is followed by *parallel play*, which can be seen when older toddlers play side by side, each doing a similar imitative activity, such as washing dolls, but without true communication or cooperation.

The next stage of play, near age three, is *cooperative play*, in which the children work on one task, sharing materials. Two children might build a garage with blocks or work together to create a sand city. Later, after much experience with other children, we begin to see the development of highly valued *sociodramatic play*. This is the dress-up and make-believe role play that adults find so appealing during the preschool to kindergarten years (ages 3-7).

Young children learn to understand social roles through role playing mommy, daddy, doctor, grocer or fire fighter.

Finally, near the beginning of middle childhood (ages 7-11) and the beginning of formal schooling, the child acquires the ability to play *games-with-rules*. These include competitive games (sports and board games) and mental games (word games and those often played in the car while traveling). *See Fig. A.*

The Value of Play for Emotional Development

Young children, whose language is limited, are better able to express their feelings and understand their world through play rather than complicated words. The child who has had a highly emotional negative experience (trip to the dentist) or positive experience (birthday party) can retreat to his or her play world and play out "dentist" or "birthday". This replaying in the safe world of play allows the child to digest both pleasurable and unpleasant experiences, to better understand them, and to begin to gain some control over his or her feelings related to the emotional experiences.

The Value of Play for Intellectual Development

Learning is not a simple process of "putting information into" the child and then having the child "put it out". The child must play with the new information in order to understand it. Children use toys and gestures symbolically in play as attempts to understand objects and experiences in their real world.

The symbols seen in children's play and artworks indicate the development of the ability to use representation (one thing stands for another). Just as a block can symbolize or represent a truck for the four- or five-year-old child, the letters *c-a-t* will represent the animal that says "meow" to the older, schoolage child. The young child needs many experiences of playing with symbols (pretending the block is a CB radio) before he or she is ready to unlock the world of words (the letters *c-a-t* stand for the animal: cat), and this is required for success in beginning reading.

It is during the preschool years that the child is moving from the make-believe symbols in play to the world of words in reading and writing. The activities in this book will help the child to bridge the process.

The Value of Play for Physical Development

It is through *sensorimotor play* (play with the senses and muscles) that the infant or toddler discovers his or her own body and its abilities. The preschool child is still developing this awareness through both small muscle activity (getting hands and eyes to work together) and large muscle activity (crawling, walking, running, balancing, and climbing).

It is also through play with the body senses of taste, smell, touch, sight, and hearing that body feelings become coordinated and useful for testing and gathering information about the world. The sensorimotor play of preschool children helps them master both understanding of their bodies and the ability to control the use of their bodies more effectively.

Social Play Development

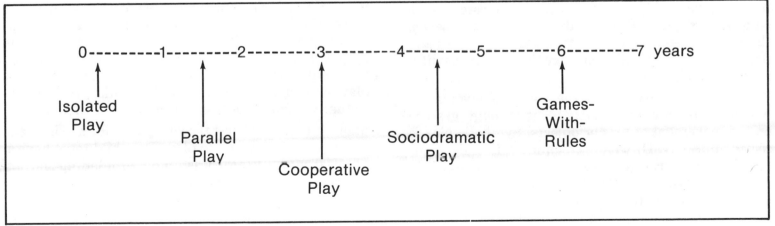

Fig. A

chapter 1   What is Play?

Play, broadly defined, is an activity engaged in for the purpose of enjoyment. The play of children helps them to understand and master their feelings and to practice and master new intellectual, social and physical skills.

In order to discuss and effectively use play activities, it becomes important that you understand the terms used to describe the various forms of play.

Sensorimotor play (SM) is the free movement of small and large muscles and the exploring of body senses to give the body practice with its sensorimotor functions. Some examples of sensorimotor play would include a young child making countless mud pies or riding endless hours on a tricycle.

In the development of sensorimotor play, the young three year old still needs a great deal of time and space for sensorimotor practice. As the other forms of play develop (sociodramatic and construction), the preschooler seems to need to devote less time to body practice. This need continues to lessen as the child grows older. Finally, around the age of seven, these motor activities begin to be tied with rules and become the middle childhood (ages 7-11) "games-with-rules" type of play.

Symbolic play (SP) is the make-believe play in which children express their ideas through gesture on the movement of toys or objects. Symbolic play is sociodramatic (SD) when the child: (1) undertakes a make-believe role (or uses a toy) and expresses it in imitative actions and/or language; (2) uses toys, unstructured materials, movements, or verbal declaration as substitutions for real objects; (3) engages in make-believe with actions and situations—verbal descriptions are substituted for actions and situations. (For example: "I'll save you"; "Come"; "I'll pick you up." or "So that's what's wrong with the engine—round part goes 'chug', 'chug'!"); (4) persists in role play—the child stays with a single role or related roles for most of a five-minute time period; (5) interacts with at least one other player within the framework of the sociodramatic play episode; and (6) verbally communicates—there is some verbal interaction related to a sociodramatic play episode. (Smilansky, 1968; Wolfgang, 1977)

The development of symbolic play begins around the age of two, when we first see the toddler pretending to "drink from a cup", or "speak on the telephone", and it makes up a large part of a three year old's play. The child begins to express his or her ideas in symbolic "make-believe play" with toys and objects. For the three year old, symbolic play is generally seen in the form of parallel play and sometimes in simple dramatic play. A four year old can usually do sociodramatic play (SD), which is more complex and shows a wider scope of roles as the child moves through ages four, five, and six. Finally, at schoolage, the child begins to give up make-believe play and incorporates make-believe into what he reads and writes. The ability to play symbolically changes as the child grows intellectually during the first seven years of life.

Stage 1 (age 2): First the young toddler needs a real object with which to play. The child must have a real cup, although he is simply pretending and not really drinking from a cup.

Stage 2 (2-2½ years): The older toddler can use a object which is similar in shape to the real object being symbolized. A circular block can be used as a substitute for a cup.

Stage 3 (2½-3 years): Now the child can use any object, regardless of the shape or purpose, to substitute for the real object. For example, a child can pick up wooden letters and pretend, "This is the mommy and this is the daddy."

Stage 4 (3-3 1/3 years): At the beginning of nursery school, the child often does not need an object for pretending. He can hold up his hands "as if" he is drinking from a cup and can go on to feed his doll or himself. This is an intellectual challenge for the child and shows developmental growth.

Stage 5 (3½-4 years): Gradually the preschooler begins to add other children to his play and is able with experience and parallel intellectual growth to engage in sociodramatic play. That is, the child can (1) take on a make-believe role, (2) pretend with objects, (3) pretend with actions, (4) persist in role play, (5) interact with at least one other child, and (6) verbally communicate. *See Fig. B.*

Symbolic Development

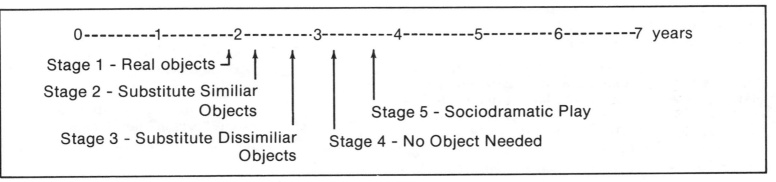

Fig. B

Understanding these developmental stages of symbolic growth permit us to evaluate the symbolic level at which children are using toys in their play. If you were to use the chart shown below, you would have a record of the child's symbolic play development. *See Fig. C.*

Symbolic Play Record

Child's Name	Stage 1	Stage 2	Stage 3	Stage 4	Stage 5
	Real Object	Similiar Object	Dissimiliar Object	No Object	Sociodramatic Play
Alice	*				
Ben					
Cicily					

Fig. C   *Add Dates   9

Keeping a record of the child's use of symbols in his or her play will enable you to evaluate the child's progress through those stages. When you introduce real objects into the environment, introduce them for Stage 1, *even with older children* who may need to recapitulate the process or who may have gone through Stage 1 at an earlier age; then encourage their movement to higher levels of symbolic play. A new riding toy might be introduced to a group of preschoolers as a "truck". Younger children may continue to play with it as just a truck, whereas older preschoolers may soon be using it as a school bus, a dune-buggy or UFO. Your role, then, is to give a wide variety of props and support with a variety of teaching behaviors (see Teacher Behavior Continuum, pages 15-17) to help the child develop these symbolic abilities.

Construction (CN) is the making of symbolic products by using materials, such as paints, paper, clay, and a wide array of similar art materials. The symbols within the product grow, develop and become more detailed and elaborated as the child grows intellectually and gains more skills with the materials. Because of the symbols used, construction is considered a form of representational play.

The child's symbolic growth can also be evaluated through art activities, a form of construction play. If you look closely at the product the child produces in such construction as finger painting, easel painting, clay, and so on, you will find symbol development. As an example, look at the key symbols that develop in drawing or painting. (These ages are a guide; they are approximate, not rigid.)

1-2 years: Random Scribbling: The child uses random scribble marks simply as a sensorimotor activity.

2-2½ years: Controlled Scribbling: The child begins to develop some control of his fine motor abilities, and scribbles gain some direction and control. After some experience with controlled scribbling, you may hear a child name his picture a "motorcycle" or a "big wheel", although there appears to be no resemblance. This is an intellectual accomplishment for the child and an indication that he is beginning his first step toward representational thinking.

2½-3 years: The Face: The next major development is for the circle to become a face.

3½-4 years: Arms and Legs: The circle "person" develops stick arms and legs, which at first lack a body, as the "appendages" stick out of the face.

4 years: The Body Appears: The human figure begins to acquire a body. Gradually, more and more body parts are added (hands, feet, hair, ears, etc.).

5 years: Floating House. First "house" drawings usually resemble a face, with windows placed like eyes and the door is like a mouth. These first houses are usually somewhere in the middle of the picture and seem to be floating in space.

5½-6 years: House on Bottom Line: Next, the bottom of the paper is used as a base line and house rests on it.

5½-6 years: Base Line Supports House in Drawing: A base line appears within the drawing and the house rests on it.

6-7 years: Two-dimensional Drawing: The base line begins to take on the quality of a horizon, which indicates the child's awareness of two-dimensional space.

The human figure, which evolves into the face-like house, is given as an example above and does appear as such in many children's symbolic development. However, each child will express the symbolic objects that are most meaningful for him or her and some might not draw the human figure or house. What is important to understand is that no matter what symbols children draw, they will progress with experience and intellectual growth through very similar development and changes. Therefore, when you are keeping a record on symbolic development in construction (artwork), you should sketch in the symbol of interest to the particular child. *See Fig. D.*

Symbolic Development In Construction

Name	*Carrie*	Date 6/10/79	Date 12/8/79	Date 11/4/80	Date 5/26/81	Date 1/9/82	Date 12/3/82

Fig. D

You will find it helpful to save samples of the child's products over a period of many weeks. Mark them with the date and place them in sequence so that you will have a concrete record of the child's symbolic development.

Three-dimensional materials, such as clay, follow a similar line of development. In working with clay, expect to see (1) random pounding, (2) controlled pounding, (3) rolling clay into snake-like rolls and later into circles, (4) adding of pieces to the rolls and circles (facial features and body parts), (5) combining products, such as people in cars or boy on a horse.

Development in three-dimensional art could also be sketched in the child's chart to keep a record of his progress in the use of that particular media.

Game-with-Rules (GWR) requires socially agreed upon rules to hold together the cooperative play. Since most preschoolers do not yet have the intellectual ability to understand the point of view of others, they usually are unable to engage productively in games with rules which involve other participants. Only the most simple games with rules, such as Lotto, are included in this collection.

11

Play and Its Development

The play of children during the preschool years will change in its complexity and duration as the child matures socially, emotionally, intellectually, and physically. The young three year old will have some success with construction using media such as crayons or paints, but will find working with clay, or three-dimensional media difficult. This will change as the child matures and gains experience and mastery over materials. (The chart below should be viewed as a hypothetical representation of 100% of the child's play capacities between ages 3-7.) *See Fig. E.*

The central goal of the play activities in this book is to help the young child develop his/her symbolic abilities both in symbolic play and construction. This will lay the foundation for the schoolage transition from symbols to words and the ability to understand and use school skills successfully.

The Developmental Play Capacities of Young Children

Age				
3	Sensorimotor		Symbolic (Parallel)	Construction
4	Sensorimotor		Symbolic (Sociodramatic)	Construction
5	Sensorimotor		Symbolic (Sociodramatic)	Construction
6	Sensorimotor		Symbolic (Sociodramatic)	Construction
7	Sensorimotor (Games-with-rules)	Symbolic (Drama) *Symbols* in play to *signs* in reading		Construction (Movement to "work")

Fig. E   25%   50%   75%   100%

Materials for Construction Play (Fluid to Structured)

Materials used by young children to produce products which show their symbolic development are often very challenging for them to master and control. We, therefore, suggest placing the materials on a continuum from fluid to structured materials. *See Fig. F.*

Materials on the fluid end of the continuum are more difficult to control. The materials on the structured end are usually easier to control. Providing a wide array of materials along this continuum enables the child to gain mastery over many challenging experiences and develop symbolic thought.

Play Material Continuum (Fluid to Structured)

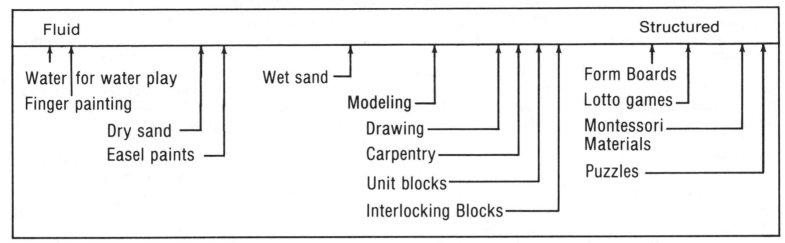

Fig. F

Fluids

Materials, such as water, finger paints, dry sand, easel paints, wet sand, clay or flour and water dough, and crayons or pens can be thought of as fluid materials. They seem by their natural form to encourage the child to explore them through sensorimotor play. But to produce symbolic construction and products, the child must control or master the materials. The child must deliberately structure the materials to his or her liking. After starting with the use of brush and paints on the paper (sensorimotor), the child next moves through the stages of symbolic development: Stage 1 *(Random Scribbling)*, Stage 2 *(Controlled Scribbling)*, Stage 3 *(Circle)*—to the stages of two- and, later, three-dimensional drawing (see pages 10-11). This type of progress occurs with most of the fluids, with the exception of water and dry sand.

As the materials appear on the continuum, from left to right (from fluid to structured), they become easier to control and master. For example, dry sand is quite fluid but if we add water, it becomes less fluid—easier to form into a shape such as a castle.

Drawing is the most structured of the fluid materials, as crayons on paper are easier for the child to control. The goal of this book is for the child to play with and master all these materials and to develop symbolic abilities within each.

Structured Materials

The materials placed on the right of the continuum are the structured materials. They basically maintain their shape and, at the most structured end, have a particular use or "one way they should be used." Often the symbols are built in. For example, puzzles have a set form and can be used in one way. As you move to the more open end of structured materials on the continuum, the materials begin to have a less clearly defined use. The child begins to structure and change the materials to fit his or her own symbolic ideas. For example, blocks, the least structured of the structured materials, maintain their shape, form and size, but the child can work with these "givens" and arrange the material to make any symbolic product

13

he or she may wish to create. You will see similar symbolic growth in the use of less structured material that you have seen in the fluids. Block play will first be random, then controlled, and eventually more elaborate.

The most structured materials will limit symbolic development, so it will be necessary to lead the child into more advanced or elaborate Lotto games, Montessori materials, form boards or puzzles.

Symbolic Material

Another group of materials to support children's play is called symbolic material, including both micro (small) and macro (large) materials. These are the materials and toys that encourage make-believe play. The micro (small) symbol toys include such items as small people figures, zoo and farm animals, small playhouses and furniture, small vehicles, puppets, and other toys that are generally used in "hand play".

In the micro-world of toys, the child can create elaborate "make-believe" dramatic episodes.

The macro (or large) symbol toys and equipment would include such items as housekeeping equipment of all kinds (stoves, iron, ironing board, sink, refrigerator); costume boxes for dress-up clothing; toy luggage; toy telephones; and larger dolls. The large equipment permits the child to develop symbol play into sociodramatic play with other children in the larger classroom space. *See Fig. G.*

It pays to have on hand a well-balanced supply of materials for construction that would range from fluid to structured, as well as abundant symbolic materials, both micro and macro. Finally, the amount of each will depend on the age level of the children. Keep in mind that the materials should parallel the amount of sensorimotor play, symbolic play, and construction play seen in Fig. E.

Fluid, Structured, and Symbolic Materials

The list is provided to give examples. Many other materials may and should be added to the list.

Fluids

Water play toys; bubble set; finger painting materials; clay on wooden clay board; sand & sand toys; sand or water table with aluminum or plastic measuring cups, hand water pump, siphon, hose, funnels, sand tools, can and sifter set, unbreakable, small family figures and animals, balances, boats, scoops, double easels with nonspill paint pots and smocks; felt-tip markers, colored chalk, wax crayons

Structured

Inlay puzzles; matching games; hammer, nails, and soft wood with work bench, unit blocks, giant blocks, play planks; scissors, variety of paper, paste, paper punch, felt pieces, bits of cloth, bits of wood, yarn, pipe cleaners; typewriter; manipulatives (string and beads, sewing basket, chunky nuts, pegboard, lacing boards); interlocking blocks, sorting boards and box for shape, color, and size; simple card games; dominoes and number boards or games; stand-up mirrors

Symbolic

Micro

washable, unbreakable doll for dressing and undressing; assorted floor blocks with small family figures; farm and zoo animal sets; puppets; animal families; wooden vehicles; table blocks; open-top doll house, including furniture and people

Macro

housekeeping equipment of all kinds; costume box for "dress-up" clothes; toy luggage; steering wheel; ride-a-stick horse; sheet or blanket for play tent; large cartons for making stores, houses, gas stations, and for climbing into; rocking chair; large cuddly toy animals; dolls of all types; doctor equipment; plastic food; balance scales; cash register and play money; variety of hats; toy telephones

Fig. G

chapter 2

Teacher Behavior Continuum (TBC)

Usually adults do not belong in the child's play world, and often you can be most helpful by maintaining a supportive stance by looking on. However, if the child does not play, or if the play is stereotypic (abnormally repetitive), you may gradually move up the Teacher Behavior Continuum to use the least controlling behavior necessary to facilitate the play activity. *See Fig. H.*

Teacher Behavior Continuum (TBC)

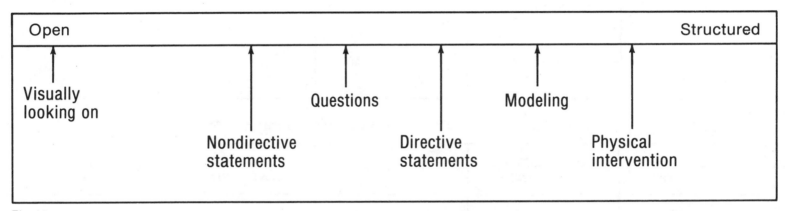

Fig. H

The Teacher Behavior Continuum (TBC) is a way of viewing your actions of getting into and out of the child's play. You may move back and forth on the Continuum. You can begin at the open end and move to the structured end, especially when you believe the child is competent. If you anticipate the child will have great difficulty with a task, you will start with the structured intervention of modeling and physical help and gradually move back along the Continuum to less control. It is your responsibility to evaluate and choose the amount of control needed that will best support the child's attempts.

The TBC provides a framework for deciding on the types of interventions appropriate to the child's play ability. When the child is in control and playing well, less teacher structure is required, and the more "open" behaviors of visually looking and nondirective statements are most appropriate. However, when a child is having great difficulty controlling his or her play, the more structured behaviors of directive statements and physical intervention may be needed.

Examples of using the TBC with each type of play activity are given in the charts on pages 16 and 17.

The Teacher Behavior Continuum with Sensorimotor Play

VISUALLY LOOKING ON	NONDIRECTIVE STATEMENTS	QUESTIONS	DIRECTIVE STATEMENTS	PHYSICAL INTERVENTION
The adult engages in supportive looking to encourage the child in the use of equipment and is ready to provide help if needed.	1. The adult verbally mirrors the child's actions. (Examples: "You're walking with your hands out for balance." "You like to walk all the way to the end and then come back.") 2. The adult helps develop concepts by using such descriptive words as: fast, slow, long, short, over, under, between.	1. The adult uses questions to challenge the child to explore new ideas and skills. (Examples: "How many different ways could you go across the beam?" "What could you carry across the beam?")	1. The adult helps the child who is having some difficulty with a task by direct instruction. (Examples: "Place your foot here and your hand here." "You need to wait for Billy to finish before you begin.")	1. The adult physically moves the child's body while modeling the proper action. (Example: You physically help the child who cannot walk backwards on the balance beam as another child demonstrates how to do it.)

The Teacher Behavior Continuum with Symbolic Play

VISUALLY LOOKING ON	NONDIRECTIVE STATEMENTS	QUESTIONS	DIRECTIVE STATEMENTS	PHYSICAL INTERVENTION
The adult does supportive looking to encourage children to play out a variety of fantasies which might potentially be frightening—the adult stands by to assist those children who get overexcited or lost in a fantasy.	The adult verbally mirrors the beginning play actions of the child. (Example: "I see you have the dishes and are ready to set the table.")	The adult uses questions to encourage children to play out and further develop fantasy themes. (Example: "Now that the table is set, what's going to happen next?")	The adult helps the children select, start or further develop their play themes by directly assigning roles. ("You're the mommy." "You're the doctor.") or by directly describing a new development in their play theme. (Example: "Now that you've finished setting the table, the doorbell rings and the mail carrier has a special delivery letter.")	The adult introduces a new prop to encourage further play or assumes a part and inserts him/herself into the play. (Example: You pick up the telephone and call the doctor.)

The Teacher Behavior Continuum With Construction

VISUALLY LOOKING ON	NONDIRECTIVE STATEMENTS	QUESTIONS	DIRECTIVE STATEMENTS	PHYSICAL INTERVENTION
The adult provides the materials and supportively looks on to encourage the child to freely and creatively use the materials.	1. The adult supports the child's efforts in using art media through such statements as, "You're working hard." 2. The adult verbally mirrors the concepts found in the child's construction. (Examples: "You're using blue." "You've made a circle." "You've added ears to your person.")	The adult uses questions to have the child verbally describe the concepts in his product. (Examples: "Can you tell me about your drawing?" "Is there a story in your drawing?" "What have you made with your clay?")	The adult helps the child to control materials or equipment with which he is having difficulty by using directive statements such as: "Keep the paint on the paper." "Brushes are used this way."	The adult helps the child develop his construction abilities by providing direct physical experiences, such as feeling a tree before drawing one or providing a model for the child's clay animal construction or having a pet visit the classroom.

Each play activity is keyed to let you know the types of play in which the child will be engaged.

You will find a box situated in the top, right-hand corner of each activity. In the box will be any of the following abbreviations:

SM   SP   CN   SD   representing the following:

CN = Construction
SM = Sensorimotor
SP = Symbolic Play
SD = Sociodramatic

Sociodramatic play, as explained on pages 8 and 9, is a very vital part of Symbolic Play. Due to its importance in the world of the child, activities that present dramatic play are keyed SD along with SP.

chapter 3

Sensorimotor Activities

Young children develop a beginning sense of identity through early play by using bodies. Young children cherish their bodies and have an inner drive to know all about themselves. Through physical movement and testing the world through their senses and body parts, children come to learn as much as possible about their world and their ability to have an impact on it. The activities which follow help the young child develop a sense of self through body awareness play, and provide the child with ways to distinguish how he is unique as a person. The child will learn to label body parts and understand how the different parts of his body can be used, while at the same time he will be developing intellectual skills of recall and classification.

mirror simon says

Goals: Helping child to:

1. Develop an awareness of his facial parts
2. Control his facial movements
3. Build a self-confidence by knowing more about himself

Objective: To be able to make facial expressions as "Simon" (you or a child leader) says

Materials: Mirror

Procedure:

1. One child or small group of children face a mirror.
2. Children make facial expressions matching whatever "Simon" says. (For example, Simon says, "Make a happy face..., be afraid..., frown..., look surprised.")
3. Let each child have a turn as Simon.

Observing Progress: Is the child able to imitate all expressions?   Is he able to imitate actions of others?

Follow-up: Have child, facing mirror, make expressions in response to short selections of music which can make him feel happy, sad, afraid, and so on.

copy cat

KEY: SM

Goals: Helping child to:

1. Identify body parts of self and others
2. Move body parts separately and then together
3. Build self-confidence by knowing more about himself

Objective: To increase awareness of other people and himself by imitating movements of a leader

Materials: None

Procedure:

1. Two players (two children or you and child) stand facing each other.
2. The leader assumes a pose (such as hands on hips).
3. The child imitates.

Observing Progress: Can child follow movements of others

- when both arms do the same things?
- when one arm or leg is in a different position from the other?
- when several parts of the body are used at once?
- when the position is changed from standing to sitting to lying?

Can the child initiate movement for others to follow?

Follow-up: Have a child take the place of the leader, initiating various poses.

Adapted with permission from Play the Perceptual Motor Way, by J.V. Akerman. Special Child Publications. Seattle, 1975.

swat the mosquito

Goals: Helping child to:

1. Become aware of his own size and shape
2. Control his body movements
3. Build self-confidence by knowing more about himself

Objective: To locate body parts without looking for them first

Materials: A pointer (ruler or pencil with eraser will do)

Procedure:

1. Child closes his eyes.
2. Leader (you or child) touches a part of the child's body with the eraser end of a pencil.
3. Child swats his body at the point of contact.
4. Child names the body part either as or immediately after he hits it.

(This activity can be done in front of a mirror.)

Observing Progress: Was the child able to swat his body parts without first looking?

Was he able to enter into the spirit of the game without becoming unduly aggressive or remaining passive?

Follow-up: Use a puppet. Have the child initiate action on another person by calling out a part of the body for the puppet to touch.

Adapted with permission from Play the Perceptual Motor Way, by J.V. Akerman. Special Child Publications. Seattle, 1975.

corner kickball

KEY: SM

Goals:
Helping child to:

1. Receive visual images and translate them into movement

2. Improve timing of movement necessary to kick a ball

3. Increase self-confidence in school and play situations where large motor and ball handling skills are necessary

Objective:
To kick a stationary ball which is placed in front of the child's foot.

Materials:
Ten-inch rubber ball

Procedure:

1. Child stands about ten feet away from and facing a corner.

2. A large ball is placed on the floor.

3. The child kicks the ball, trying to hit the wall so the ball will bounce back.

4. Several children can play. Whoever catches the ball, kicks it.

Observing Progress:
Is the child able to kick the ball, properly timing his movement and that of the ball?

Follow-up:
Modify activity by setting up "pins" (empty plastic milk bottles) near the corner to knock over.

Adapted with permission from Play the Perceptual Motor Way, by J.V. Akerman. Special Child Publications. Seattle, 1975.

people puzzles

Goal: Helping child to:

1. Develop body awareness and body concepts

Objectives:

1. To name parts of the body as represented by the puzzle pieces
2. To relate puzzle parts to his own body

Materials: Picture puzzles of people with separate, single pieces for main body parts

Procedure:

1. Name and discuss function of body parts.
2. Have child talk about the parts of his body as he is putting the puzzle together.

Observing Progress: Was the child familiar with his own body parts and their names and functions?

Was he comfortable working with structured materials?

Follow-up: Have one child trace another's outline on butcher paper or large paper bags. Encourage the child to tell about his own parts.

obstacle course

Goals: Helping child to:

1. Improve skills in locomotion
2. Judge distance and depth correctly
3. Make decisions
4. Improve self-confidence and self-concept
5. Verbalize alternatives

Objectives:

1. To improve ability to run, climb, crawl and hop by moving over, under, around and through objects
2. To make decisions based on body size and body awareness as the body relates to the objects

Materials: Objects, such as chairs, cardboard boxes, barrels, milk cartons, ropes, ladders, tires

Procedure:

1. Set up obstacle course indoors or out.
2. Children (with your help as necessary) decide what players must do when they get to each object. Jump over it? Run around it? Crawl under it?
3. Children try to go through course as fast as possible without upsetting the objects.
4. Another challenge would be for children to try going through the course without touching objects or using their hands.

Observing Progress: Check the skills the child is able to do efficiently. Those unchecked would need to be developed.

Rolling ____ Crawling ____ Walking ____ Running ____ Jumping ____ Galloping ____ Hopping ____ Skipping ____ Leaping ____

Did the children react positively to their bodies when they engaged in the activity? Negatively? Why?

Follow-up: Have child set up obstacle course for others giving directions as to the method of moving through course.

Adapted with permission from Play the Perceptual Motor Way, by J.V. Akerman. Special Child Publications. Seattle, 1975.

hand & footprints to keep

KEY SM CN

Goals: Helping child to:
1. Understand his own uniqueness
2. Become more aware of his own size and shape

Objective: To make handprint and/or footprint plaques

Materials: Clay, one-pound coffee can, pencil, plastic straw, ribbon, glaze, access to an electric kiln

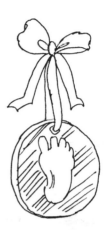

Procedure:
1. Using an empty coffee can, cut circles out of clay which has been rolled to about ¾" thickness. Allow two circles for each child.
2. Have the child press his foot firmly and evenly in the center of one circle, his hand in the center of the other.
3. With a pencil or stylus, print the year.
4. With a straw, punch a hole completely through the clay about ½" from the top edge.
5. Allow the clay to dry.
6. Bisque fire.
7. Glaze by dipping or brushing.
8. Fire again.
9. When completed, allow the child to compare his handprint to a friend's by placing his hand in the print on one of his friend's plaques.

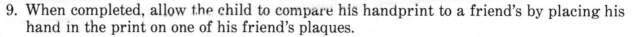

Observing Progress: Did the activity help the child understand his own physical uniqueness? Was he pleased with the product made?

Follow-up: Wrap plaques for presents to parents or grandparents. Introduce or encourage child to make simple designs with clay or play dough.

Adapted with permission from Play the Perceptual Motor Way, by J.V. Akerman. Special Child Publications. Seattle, 1975.

silhouette

Goals: Helping child to:

1. Understand that his physical features are generally like those of others, but some features have special and unique characteristics
2. Recognize the distinct differences that make him a unique individual

Objectives:

1. For you to create a silhouette of the child, which he glues onto white posterboard
2. For the child to recognize his unique "silhouette" from a group of several

Materials: One sheet 12" x 18" newsprint, one sheet 12" x 18" black construction paper, masking tape, projector or bright light, pencil, white posterboard or tagboard

Procedure:

1. Tape newsprint on the wall at the level of the child's head.
2. Seat child on chair or stool.
3. Shine a bright light on the child.
4. Draw carefully around the shadow created.
5. Staple newsprint silhouette onto black construction paper.
6. Cut out both sheets. Discard newsprint.
7. Paste the black silhouette on the white posterboard with rubber cement or glue. (The child may do this part of the activity with your careful supervision.)
8. After discussing and pointing out differences in features, allow child to pick out his own silhouette and that of a friend's.
9. Let the child send the silhouette to someone special—a family member or a friend.

Observing Progress: Was the child able to pick out his own silhouette or that of a friend's?

Could he spot distinguishing features, such as hair, nose or chin shape.

Follow-up: Read (or better yet, tell) the poem "Mirror Games". Act out the action in the poem. Ask child to do the same.

Mirror Games

Mirror, mirror,
On the wall,
Who's that person,—
Who shall I call?

My mouth smiles,
So does his.
When my brow frowns,
His frowns! Gee whiz!

My hands go up
His do, too.
I bend down,
He touches his shoe.

I clap my hands
And tap my toe.
He does the same—
How does he know?

I hide, he hides—
How can it be?
The secret's out—
That he is me!

—Mary Ellen Wolfgang

pretzel

Goals: Helping child to:

1. Increase his awareness of himself and others
2. Understand how his body can move
3. Control his body movements

Objective: To know how one part can relate to another part of the body

Materials: None

Procedure:

1. Someone is appointed "The Leader".
2. The leader assumes a position which involves body parts meeting, such as elbow on knee, thumb on heel, or wrist on ankle.
3. The child imitates the position.

Observing Progress: Can the child form the same position as the leader? Does he exhibit self-confidence in knowing about himself?

Follow-up: Continue the above activity by

- taking turns, letting the child think of a position to be imitated.
- touching without using hands, such as ear on shoulder.

a pointing song

Goals: Helping child to:

1. Identify own body parts
2. Move body parts together
3. Become more aware of his own size and shape
4. Control body movements
5. Build self-confidence by knowing more about himself

Objective: To improve ability to name body parts

Materials: Tune for "There Is a Tavern in the Town"

Procedure: Point to the body parts as you sing:

"Head, shoulders, knees and toes, knees and toes,

"Head, shoulders, knees and toes, knees and to - o - o - es,

"Eyes and ears and mouth and nose,

"Head, shoulders, knees and toes, knees and toes!"

Observing Progress: Did the child name parts of the body? Did he participate freely in song and actions?

Follow-up: Use "An Action Song" (page 30) for follow-up to "A Pointing Song".

an action song

Goals: Helping child to:

1. Identify body parts
2. Understand how the body can move and what each part does
3. Control his body movements
4. Build self-confidence by knowing more about himself

Objective: To increase knowledge of what action each body part can perform as evidenced by responding to directions given in a song

Materials: Tune for "Skip to My Lou"

Procedure: While singing, do the actions of the song.

- Sing line 1.
- Sing or hum and do actions for lines 2 and 3.
- Sing line 4.

  "Clap, clap, clap your hands
  (action), (action), (action) your hands

  Clap, clap, clap your hands
  Early in the morning."

Other actions may be used to involve other parts of the body:

Stamp your feet...

Nod your head...

Swing your arms...

Blink your eyes...

Hop around...

Join your hands...

Observing Progress: Does the child know the names of body parts?

Is he able to move in an uninhibited but controlled manner?

chapter

Fluid Activities

Fluids include such materials as water, finger paints, sand, easel, clay and drawing equipment. These materials help child to develop physically through practicing large and small muscle coordination. Intellectually, fluids help the child to practice understanding quantity and transformations (for instance: two ounces of clay is the same amount whether rolled in a ball or a sausage). Fluids also assist the child's emotional growth by providing an acceptable outlet for emotions (including fear, anger and happiness) and by giving the child the opportunity and challenge to grow in self-control.

paint the outdoors

Goals: Helping child to:

1. Develop sensorimotor control
2. Demonstrate symbolic and/or dramatic play through the medium of painting

Objectives: The child will:

1. Manipulate the brushes and water
2. Pretend the water is paint
3. Take on the role of a "painter"
4. Suggest to and/or take suggestions from another child about how to play with (or use) water and brushes

Materials: Pail, water, large paintbrush for each child

Procedure:

1. Fill a can or pail with water.
2. The child uses the water and large paintbrush to "paint" the outside of a building or equipment on the playground.
3. The child can work alone or in groups of two or three.

Observing Progress:

1. Did the child share materials with at least one other child?
2. Did the child talk about the water, the texture of the building or the patterns he made on on the wall?
3. Did the child pretend the water was paint, or the wall was something else?

Follow-up: Sing to the tune of "This Is the Way We Wash Our Hands": *This is the way we paint our fence...,paint our school..., and so on.*

sinking and floating

Goals: Helping child to:

1. Develop an awareness of natural environment
2. Discover the natural characteristics of water
3. Experiment and test hypotheses

Objectives:

1. Given certain objects, the child will be able to discuss with others which ones float and which ones sink
2. After experimentation, the child will be able to intelligently guess which types of objects sink and which float

Materials: Tub, water, toy boat, paper, plastic, sponge, soap, metal, a bottle (capped and uncapped)

Procedure:

1. Fill tub halfway to top with water.
2. Let child guess first whether a certain object will float or sink.
3. Place objects one at a time on the water to see if they float or sink.
4. Make generalization about certain types of objects after experimentation is done.

Observing Progress: Determine if child:

1. Played in a controlled, but uninhibited manner
2. Worked alone or with others
3. Was able to use experimentation to come to a conclusion

Follow-up: Add a dash of dishwashing soap to the water and give the child an eggbeater.

bubble blowing

Goals: Helping child to:

1. Develop awareness of his physical world
2. Experiment and test hypotheses

Objectives:

1. Given water and soap, or soapy solution, the child will be able to blow bubbles
2. On a windy day, child will let the wind blow the bubbles away

Materials: Very soapy bubble solution made of Ivory soap chipped in pieces and allowed to stand overnight, wire bubble blowers or empty wooden thread spools. (A bar of soap and a cup of water works well, also. Dip spool in water and touch to soap before blowing gently through other end.)

Procedure:

1. Using bubble solution and spool, allow child to experiment freely outdoors. If he sucks in instead of blowing out, demonstrate and/or tell him to blow gently through the spool after dipping it into the bubble solution.
2. If it is a windy day, encourage the child to let the wind "blow" bubbles. If there is no wind, child can quickly move his arm through the air thereby creating his own "wind".

Observing Progress: Was child able to blow bubbles and not suck in?

Did he participate freely in the activity?

Did he interact with his peers?

KEY SM
SP

Follow-up: • Make "frozen bubbles" outdoors in very cold weather.

1. Dip spool into bubble solution.

2. Hold finger over spool to keep bubble there. Bubble will freeze very quickly.

• Share the following poem with the children:

Bubbles, Bubbles, Bubbles

I blew some pretty bubbles,
  They danced in the air.
I watched them floating higher
  'Til POOF! they were not there.
Where did my bubbles go, oh where?

—*Josephine Newbury*

More Kindergarten Resources, by Josephine Newbury
Copyright John Knox Press 1974
Used by permission.

kaleidoscope painting

KEY SM CN

Goals: Helping child to:

1. Understand that two colors make another color (blue and yellow make green)

2. Develop small muscle coordination used in folding

3. Improve self-concept by successfully making colored tissue paper

Objectives: To create a "painting" by dipping folded paper into colored water

Materials: Food coloring, muffin tin, water, tissue paper which has been cut into squares or rectangles, newspaper

Procedure: The child will:

1. Fold tissue paper into a very small square, rectangle, or triangle.

2. Put a different food color in each cup of the muffin tin. (Keep some colors full strength, dilute some with water.)

3. Dip each corner of the tissue into a food color.

4. Place folded paper quickly between layers of newspaper.

5. Step on newspaper with foot to press water out.

6. Unfold tissue.

7. Let dry.

Observing Progress: Did child comprehend and show how some colors are made? Was he successful in folding and dipping? Did he use verbal language during the activity?

Follow-up:
- Use dyed tissue as a display background.
- Letters can be cut out of tissue paper and used to spell the child's name.
- Read *Little Blue & Little Yellow*, by Leo Leonni. (See Bibliography.)

wagon wash

Goals: Helping child to:
1. Discover characteristics of water
2. Develop play interaction with others
3. Develop large muscle coordination
4. Discover that washing things makes them clean

Objectives:
1. To clean wagons and tricycles
2. To communicate verbally with others during activity

Materials: Wagons, tricycles, buckets, soap, water, rags or sponges

Procedure: With materials at hand, child or group of children wash wagons and/or tricycles. This activity can be as simple (one child washing wagon—no verbalization) or as complex (working together, verbalizing about price to charge, etc.) as the maturity and developmental level of the child or children allow.

Observing Progress: Is the child involved in symbolic play? If not, try to think of ways you can structure this type of activity so he will be the next time.

Follow-up: Sing: "This Is the Way We Wash Our Hands"...*Cars...Tricycles...Wagons*

window washing

KEY: SM SP

Goals: Helping child to:
1. Develop large muscle skills
2. Discover characteristics of water
3. Allow for symbolic play
4. Join in a cooperative activity

Objective: Given window washing materials, child will wash windows or mirrors in and/or outside the classroom

Materials: Rag or sponge for washing, bucket, vinegar, water, paper towels or rags for drying

Procedure:
1. You must mix vinegar with water for cleaning solution.
2. Using the cleaning solution, child carefully washes windows and/or mirrors.
3. If windows are low, one child can wash the window on the outside while another child is washing on the inside.
4. Two children can work on one window—one child washes and one dries.

The quality of the work done is not a primary concern, but rather the experience of doing or participating in water play.

Observing Progress: Was the child confident in his use of water? Was symbolic play involved in isolation? with others?

Follow-up: Use the tune to "This Is the Way We Wash Our Clothes" and substitute the words *windows* or *mirrors* for clothes.

Caution: Children should be instructed about the breakability of glass and the hazardous qualities of broken glass. This activity should be monitored closely.

free expression

KEY: SM

Goals: Helping child to:

1. Enjoy being "messy"
2. Experience kinesthetic and tactile sensations
3. Engage in a large muscle activity

Objectives:

1. To provide opportunity for child to experiment with finger paints
2. To develop appreciation for form and color

Materials: Choice of paper; finger paints; laminated table, oilcloth, or newspaper

Procedure:

1. Encourage freedom to experiment by painting to music.
2. Child uses fingers, hands and arms to overlay and mix colors.
3. Encourage child to clean up after himself.

Observing Progress: Did child:

- paint lines and circles?
- blend colors?
- utilize entire sheet of paper?
- stay within paper boundary?

Follow-up: For a more structured activity:

- Child can print using half a potato, onion, lemon, or carrot slice.
- Child's hands or feet can be "printed" on paper.

For a less structured activity: water play in a wading pool.

me, myself and I

KEY: SM

Goals: Helping child to:

1. Develop large muscle coordination
2. Experience freedom of movement allowed in finger painting
3. Accept himself

Objectives:

1. To finger-paint parts of body drawn on paper
2. To name parts of body represented on painting

Materials: Large roll of brown paper, one dark-colored crayon, finger paints, newspaper

Procedure:

1. Cut roll of brown paper into large pieces, longer than each child is tall.
2. Spread out newspaper on the floor.
3. Place brown paper on newspaper.
4. Each child lies down on a piece of brown paper while you trace around him with the crayon.
5. Using the tracing as an outline, encourage the child to paint an image of himself.
6. As child paints, discuss body parts, assisting him with names and functions of each.
7. Let painting dry. Cut it out and hang for display.

Observing Progress: What comments did the child make in relation to his body?

Which children seemed to feel most self-confident based on their verbal and/or physical expression and actions?

Follow-up:

- Have a Talk-About-Ourselves Time. Display the finger paintings of each child. With a small group, discuss how we look, parts of our bodies, and what we like about our bodies.
- Sing "Hokey Pokey" from *Music for Early Childhood* (see Bibliography).

clown face

KEY: SM SP

Goals: Helping child to:

1. Become aware of his own size and shape
2. Develop small muscle coordination
3. Build self-confidence by knowing more about himself

Objectives:

1. To create his own clown face by using finger paints
2. To name parts of his face as he paints

Materials: Smock, various colors of finger paints (tempera may be used), cold cream or petroleum jelly, soap, water, washcloth and towel, hats, if desired

Procedure:

1. Have child apply small amount of cold cream or petroleum jelly to his face. (This makes paint easier to remove when finished.)
2. Encourage child to make his face look like a clown face by using finger paints, one color at a time. (A picture of a clown hanging within visual range can be helpful.) Older children (4-5) can do this activity in pairs— each making up the other.

Observing Progress: Was child able to "make" himself into a clown? Did he work in an uninhibited, but not aggressive, manner? Can child name parts of face?

Follow-up:
- Allow child to role play a clown before others.
- Place hats on heads and have a parade.

monoprints

Goals: Helping child to:
1. Use and develop muscle control
2. Discover effects of mixing colors and using various finger-painting techniques
3. Experience freedom from inhibitions
4. Experience kinesthetic and tactile sensations

Objectives:
1. To use finger paints readily and freely with fingers, whole hands, arms, and even elbows
2. To preserve child's finger-painting creation by creating a monoprint

Materials: Commercial or homemade finger paints, sponge, water, laminated desk or table

Procedure:
1. Wet tabletop with wet sponge. The use of a table rather than paper allows the child more freedom to experiment and lessens his attempts to "draw a picture". However, if you do not have a table that has a laminated top, use paper that has a gloss on one side. Tape the paper to the tabletop.
2. Put one to two tablespoons of finger paint, one color only, on the tabletop or paper.
3. Allow child to experience the medium of finger painting and by creating his own "designs".
4. Preserve child's design by placing a sheet of newsprint on top of the painting and smoothing it down carefully.
5. Lift paper, which will have a print of child's finger painting. Let dry.
6. Clean tabletop with soap and water.

Observing Progress:
- Did the child experience more freedom through the use of a tabletop or by using a very large piece of paper than when having to use a smaller piece of paper for finger painting?
- Was the child able to blend colors and create new ones?
- Was the child successful in using parts of the body other than the index finger in his painting?
- Was he involved in social interaction while painting?

Follow-up: Finger-paint to music or to poetry.

Sing to the tune of "If You're Happy and You Know It, Clap Your Hands":

*If you're happy and you know it,
finger-paint!*

*If you're happy and you know it,
finger-paint!*

*If you're happy and you know it, then
your face will surely show it.*

*If you're happy and you know it,
finger-paint!*

Verses 2-5

   ...paint with wrists (elbows, nose, toes).

Last Verse

   ...paint some more.

mirror finger painting

Goals:
Helping child to:

1. Develop large muscle coordination
2. Become aware of body parts
3. Experience freedom of working with finger paints

Objectives:

1. To use various parts of the body (arms, hands, feet, fingers, elbows) in controlled, but uninhibited manner to spread finger paints on a mirror
2. To watch one's self while painting

Materials:
Finger paints, full-length mirror (smaller one will suffice if full-length is not available), paper towels or rags, smock, bucket of water for clean up

Procedure:

1. Lay mirror flat on table or floor, or leave attached to wall. If a stand-up mirror is used, be sure it is firmly balanced or supported so it will not tip.
2. The child may be instructed to paint freely or to paint what he sees as he looks into mirror (himself).
3. Encourage child to use various parts of his body in painting.
4. Cleanup needs supervision and is a good time for child to engage in verbal interaction with you and/or peers.

Observing Progress:
Was the child comfortable with this activity?

Were his movements controlled but uninhibited?

Follow-up:
Barefoot printing on the floor is always fun. Allow children to dip feet in pan of water and walk or run on brown paper which has been taped to the floor. Play fast and slow music to stimulate "dancing".

sandbox roadways

KEY: SM CN SP SD

Goals: Helping child to:
1. Develop small muscle skills
2. Engage in role play and symbolic play

Objective: Given selection of small cars, trucks, and tractors, child will engage in sensorimotor and symbolic and/or sociodramatic play

Materials: Sandbox filled with sand, small cars, trucks, tractors. If a large sandbox is unavailable, small boxes can be used.

Procedure:
1. Encourage the child to role play "truck driver" or "garage attendant" or "race car driver" or whatever his imagination dictates.
2. If there is a group of children, allow free interaction to occur.
3. Some assistance may be needed by the younger children to begin mapping out roadways.

Observing Progress: Was the child involved in symbolic play?
Was the child involved in parallel play?
Was the child involved in sociodramatic play?

Follow-up: Allow more of the same kind of activity. Try using individual boxes filled with sand or sawdust for the more aggressive child and a large sandbox for the more passive child. Play ideas could be suggested, such as:

"Pretend you are a bus driver."

"Pretend you are a gas station attendant."

"Pretend you are working on a road."

Allow time for more sand play.

45

soil making

KEY SM CN

Goals: Helping child to:

1. Develop his imagination and curiosity
2. Develop sensorimotor skill

Objectives:

1. To make soil
2. To observe nature
3. To follow directions

Materials: Rocks (slate, shale, sandstone), leaves, water

Procedure: Child will:

1. Crush small rocks with a hammer. The rocks will look like sand when finished. (You may have to do this for younger children.)
2. Bring in decaying leaves (found under bushes or shrubs). Grind or break them up.
3. Mix broken-up rock and leaves together to form soil.
4. Compare it with soil found on the ground around the home or school.
5. Discuss uses of soil.

Observing Progress: What were the child's questions and comments? Did the child participate freely? Did the child need more experience with the dry sand medium?

Follow-up: Make a "worm farm". Dig for worms under decaying leaves. Place in moistened soil in a glass container to observe.

Caution: Close supervision is required for crushing rocks safely.

sand painting

KEY: SM

Goals: Helping child to:

1. Experiment with shape and design
2. Express himself in a controlled manner

Objective: To experiment with texture through sand painting

Materials: Sand, shaker with large holes, paper, white, all-purpose glue, large box without a lid

Procedure: This activity may be more fun if you demonstrate and then assist the child.

1. Make a line or shape by pouring glue onto the paper.
2. Place sand into the shaker.
3. Child shakes sand all over paper.
4. Shake paper carefully over the box so that excess sand falls into the box.
5. Hang up design to dry.

Observing Progress: Was the child's expression controlled? Inhibited? Did the child complete his painting?

Follow-up: Allow the child to do the activity again using colored sand, glitter, or bird seed. Feel different textures; discuss rough and smooth.

sand sorting

Goals: Helping child to:

1. Compare sizes through use of senses
2. Develop small muscle control
3. Develop eye/hand coordination
4. Develop concepts of same/different and big/little

Objective: To combine and separate various materials and textures

Materials: Plastic containers, sieves and strainers with different sized holes (for example, plastic salad strainer with large and small holes), large sandbox, sand, rice, popcorn, dried beans, pebbles, or other small objects

Procedure:

1. Provide sand and containers with various materials.
2. Discuss differences in how the materials look and feel.
3. Child will mix different materials with sand.
4. Use different sized sieves to discuss big and small.
5. Child will experiment with sifting different sized objects through various sieves.
6. Let child use fine sieves to sift out all materials except sand.

Observing Progress: Could the child identify objects and strainers by size or amount? Could the child, after some practice, match the materials to the strainers through which the material would most easily filter?

Follow-up: Stimulate creative dramatics by showing different types of strainers and suggesting that the child be different textured materials. *If you were a piece of popcorn or a grain of sand, how would you try to get through this strainer? Would you squeeze, slither, run? If you were wet, how would you get through?*

sand soup

Goals: Helping child to:

1. Learn to follow directions
2. Develop sensorimotor skill
3. Progress from sensorimotor play to symbolic and/or sociodramatic play

Objective: To make a "pretend" soup from ingredients listed below

Materials: Several cups of sand, leaves, pebbles or small rocks, grasses, flowers, old large pot or kettle, wooden spoons or sticks

Procedure: Read *Stone Soup* (see Bibliography) to the child as an introduction to activity. (It can be used for a very effective follow-up and discussion.)

1. Create a "pot of soup" using sand as the basic ingredient and other combinations as the child suggests. Remind him that this is a "pretend soup" which people do not eat.

2. Allow the child to stir. If more than one are making soup, let them take turns stirring. Some children may wish to build a make-believe fire to "cook" the soup. Be careful that it "doesn't burn".

Observing Progress: Was the child able to enter into the spirit of making "sand soup"? Was there verbal interaction? Symbolic play? Sociodramatic play?

Follow-up: Some children may want to set the table, serve the soup and feed it to their dolls. All make-believe, of course!

succulent garden

Goals:

Helping child to:

1. Understand that plants need soil, water and light

2. Learn to follow directions

3. Perform an activity in a controlled manner

Objectives:

1. To fill a container with sand

2. To plant succulents in it

Materials:

Aquarium, sand, water, cactus plants, cup

Procedure:

The child will:

1. From an outdoor sandpile or indoor sandbox, carefully gather enough sand to fill the aquarium one-half full.

2. Add about one cup water. Mix with both hands or with stick or wooden spoon.

3. Poke holes using two fingers together—one hole for each plant that is to be planted.

4. Remove the plants from their pots. (If they are in peat pots, leave as they are.)

5. Carefully set each plant in the holes in the sand, pressing down firmly around the edges.

6. Water sparingly when needed.

Observing Progress:

Was the child able to perform the activity without becoming impatient? Could the child follow your directions?

Follow-up:

Make an ant farm or a worm garden for the child to observe.

free form painting

Goals: Helping child to:

1. Experiment, explore and express feelings difficult to put into words
2. Experience motor expression
3. Give form to feelings and accept help
4. Engage in free-form expression

Objectives:

1. To spread paint
2. To make lines, circles, then forms
3. To name the painting, if desired
4. To produce a finished product

Materials: Paper, large brushes, colored paints, easel

Procedure: Allow child to explore by himself, or guide him into spatter painting, straw painting, string painting or printing.

Observing Progress:

Did the child paint lines and circles?

Did child name painting?

Did child produce recognizable symbols in painting?

Did child paint with peers?

Follow-up: Paint a mural related to something with which the child is familiar: city streets, stores, farm, playground, and so on.

bubble painting

KEY: SM

Goals: Helping child to:

1. Explore medium of soap and water
2. Gain satisfaction from water play

Objective: By blowing bubbles into soapy water, the child will be able to create painting on paper

Materials: Absorbent paper, liquid soap, water, 8″ diameter bowl, food coloring, straw

Procedure:

1. Put liquid soap and water in bowl.
2. Add coloring.
3. Give child straw and encourage him to blow as many bubbles as he can.
4. When bubbles rise over top of bowl, take piece of absorbent paper and place over bowl.
5. Design will be printed on paper with top of bowl as border.

Observing Progress: Was the child able to maintain muscle control? Did he enjoy water play?

Follow-up: Discuss other times we might experience water with bubbles. Examples: bath time, doing dishes, washing the floor.

Caution: Use plastic bowl for safety. Make sure child blows in straw and does not suck in soapy water.

magic pictures

KEY: SM

Goals: Helping child to:

1. Develop motor expression

2. Develop ways of giving form to feelings

Objective: To create a picture by drawing with crayons and spreading paint

Materials: White or yellow crayon, white paper, paint (one color), paintbrush

Procedure:

1. Draw a scribbly picture on paper using crayon. Leave clean spaces on the paper.

2. Cover the entire piece of paper with the paint. The picture will suddenly take on a whole new look.

Observing Progress: Did the child show controlled motor movements in dealing with the activity?

Follow-up: Let the child express to you or his peers what happened when he painted over the crayoned drawing.

Allow the child to experiment with, and experience, invisible ink.

stipple painting

KEY SM SP

Goals:
Helping child to:

1. Develop small muscle coordination
2. Give form to his feelings
3. Enjoy being "messy" in a controlled manner

Objective:
To create a picture using the technique of stippling

Materials:
Different colored stamp pads (see page 144 for directions on how to make stamp pads), pieces of cellulose sponge cut into small geometric shapes, newsprint or shelf paper

Procedure:
You may wish to demonstrate this activity so the child has a better understanding of what to do.

1. Press sponge lightly on print pad and then touch it to paper. (Designs may be made and colors experimented with as child overlaps prints made with sponge.)

2. Encourage child to:

- paint what he feels
- make a picture
- paint a dog, house, or person
- talk about what he is painting to you or to a friend

Observing Progress:
Was child able to complete activity using controlled muscular movements?

Did child talk with others about his painting?

Follow-up:

1. Allow child to stipple a border for a picture of himself. Have him dictate a story about himself which you write down. The story can be made into a booklet with the child's picture as the cover.
2. Winter pictures may be made by using white paint on blue or black construction paper. Stippling also makes interesting borders around other artwork.

 This activity is adapted from *More Kindergarten Resources*, by Josephine Newbury, Copyright John Knox Press, 1974. Used by permission.

string painting

KEY SM SP

Goals: Helping child to:

1. Use paint and manipulative materials in a controlled, effective manner
2. Gain pleasure and satisfaction through different techniques in controlling paint
3. Develop small muscle coordination

Objectives:

1. To create a painting using the technique of string painting
2. Using string to paint lines and/or circles

Materials: Paint stamp pads (see page 144 for directions on how to make pads), heavy cotton string 14-16 inches in length, manila paper, plastic fork

Procedure: You may wish to demonstrate this technique before the child attempts it.

1. Fold paper in half then open out flat.
2. Drop string onto paint pad and press it down with the plastic fork until it is covered with paint.
3. Place string on one side of the flat paper.

4. Fold paper over and press gently.
5. Open paper, remove string, replacing it on the paint pad.
6. Continue the process using strings of other colors. Arrange strings on paper in varied ways.

Observing Progress: Could child make lines and circles with strings? Was there any verbal interaction of the child with his peers or you while painting?

Follow-up: Draw a simple design on cardboard or a wooden block. Use the dry strings from this activity and glue them to cardboard or a block following lines of the original design. You may wish to shellac this so that it can be used for printing. Reapply paint for each print.

This technique is adapted from *More Kindergarten Resources*, by Josephine Newbury, John Knox Press, 1974. Used by permission.

blow painting

Goals: Helping child to:

1. Understand that colors can be mixed to form new colors

2. Experiment with color and design in a controlled manner

Objectives:

1. To paint by blowing air through a straw into paint on paper

2. To make designs with paint on paper

Materials: Glossy shelf paper, plastic straws, two or three primary colors of tempera paint, milk cartons or paper cups, medicine droppers

Procedure:

1. Using the medicine dropper, the child puts a drop or two of one color of paint onto the paper.

2. He then blows through the straw to make the drops move around.

3. Different colored drops can be added. The child can then blow the paints into each other, creating rivulets and thereby mixing the colors. The paint needs to be thin enough so that it can be blown easily over the paper.

Observing Progress: Did the child maintain sensorimotor control while working?

Was he able to create a new color by mixing the primary colors?

Follow-up: Make folded paper paint "blots" just for fun! Take a dropperful of paint and drop several colors onto half of the paper which has previously been folded and then opened out flat. Carefully fold paper together and then open to see what has been made.

whatever is it? printing

KEY: SM

Goals: Helping child to:
1. Communicate verbally
2. Discriminate visually
3. Express himself in controlled but uninhibited manner
4. Develop small muscle coordination and skill

Objectives:
1. To do "object printing" on paper with paint and an ordinary small object
2. To see if others can guess with what object the child painted

Materials: Any small objects which can be dipped in paint and used to print (potato masher, paper chips, empty thread spools, sticks, cardboard, brush, sponge, cut-up vegetables, such as lemons, oranges, potatoes, carrots, and green peppers), flat pans for paint, paper or cloth on which to print

Procedure:
1. Using one color and one object, child will print on paper by dipping object into paint and then onto paper over and over again.
2. After child or group has finished, allow each child to hold up his picture and ask others what object they think he used to paint with. This makes a fun guessing game.

Observing Progress: Did child successfully complete a printed paper?

Was he able to lead the game with his peers or you?

Follow-up: Play guessing game, "What Is It?"

Have pictures of well-known objects in a paper bag. Child selects a picture and verbally describes it without showing it to anyone. Other children or you try to guess the object from the child's description.

sand play

Goals: Helping child to:

1. Expand imagination
2. Progress from sensorimotor play to constructive play to symbolic play to sociodramatic play

Objective: To manipulate sand, exploring its possibilities as dry, wet and in combination with other materials such as seashells

Materials: Sand; water; props, such as trucks, shovels, buckets sifters, measuring spoons and cups, and containers

Procedure: You will:

1. Allow for freedom of movement and play.
2. Watch for ways of helping the aggressive or passive child.
3. Listen to and observe the child to gain insight into his behavior and growth.

Observing Progress: Place the date on which you observed each child involved in the specific types of play (SM, CN, SP, DP) in the boxes.

Sand Play

Name	SM	CN	SP	SD
Lisa	Sept.			
Justin	Sept.		Oct. 1	

Follow-up: Read *A Hole is to Dig* by Ruth Krauss, (Harper & Row, 1952). Make a chart which defines sand. *(Sand is to _____ .)*

outdoor gardening

KEY: SM

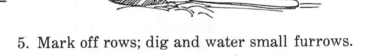

Goals: Helping child to:

1. Develop small muscle control and coordination
2. Become more aware of his environment
3. Experience physical and emotional release through working in soil and with growing things

Objective: To grow individual or group garden

Materials: Shovel, spading fork, small trowel, rake, watering can, seeds which will sprout quickly, such as lima bean, 1' x 1' plot of ground for each one or two children or larger space for entire class.

Procedure: Child will:

1. Outdoors in spring, dig up sod.
2. Dig ground well to aerate it.
3. Get rid of any large rocks.
4. Rake ground smooth.
5. Mark off rows; dig and water small furrows.
6. Sow seeds evenly.
7. Moisten with watering can.
8. Water and weed as needed during growth.

Observing Progress: During and after activity did child display sense of worth and achievement concerning the activity?

Did child work with another in planting and caring for the garden?

Follow-up:
- Let the child pretend to be gardener or farmer supplying food for table or market. Carry the play along until the child no longer has interest.
- Take photographs of the child planting seeds, caring for them, and watching them grow. Write down stories the child dictates about the seeds and make books.

BELMONT COLLEGE LIBRARY
CURRICULUM LAB

snow play

Goals: Helping child to:

1. Engage in sensorimotor play
2. Become more aware of his environment
3. Create a recognizable product

Objective: Using medium of snow and paints, create snowpeople and/or snow angels

Materials: A snowy day; snow shovel; props for snowpeople, such as hats, scarves, buttons, carrots, mittens; 1″ brushes; jars; diluted food coloring

Procedure:

1. On a snowy day, allow child to simply experience snow by touching it, running in it, lying in it.
2. After a few minutes of "free play", encourage child to:

   • make a snowman or snowlady

   • make snow angels

   Snowpeople can be dressed up with props. Snow angels can have faces and buttons painted on with diluted food coloring.

Observing Progress: Did the child participate freely in the activity?   Did he make a recognizable product?

Follow-up:

• Read to the child Ezra Jack Keats' *The Snowy Day*. Using chalk or light crayons on dark construction paper, allow the child to draw what he saw and/or did in the snow.

• Make snow ice cream.

digging for worms

KEY: SM SP

Goals: Helping child to:

1. Develop small muscle coordination

2. Stimulate awareness of environment

3. Experience physical release through digging and piling

Objective: To obtain earthworms by digging in soil

Materials: Small sturdy shovels, digging forks, an area of ground in which to dig

Procedure: Child will:

1. Dig up sod to find worms.

2. Put worms in container along with a small amount of soil and moistened leaves.

3. Add a very small amount of water occasionally. If earthworms are hard to find, you may wish to dampen an area of ground about 4' x 6' and cover it with a plastic sheet or tarp held down by rocks or bricks. Look for worms in about one week.

Observing Progress: Did the child participate freely in this activity?

Did any symbolic play or sociodramatic play occur?

Follow-up:

1. Use worms when the child goes fishing.

2. Make a worm garden for observation.

3. Plant a garden (see "Outdoor Gardening", page 59).

indoor gardening

KEY: SM

Goals: Helping child to:

1. Develop controlled sensorimotor skill
2. Understand that some foods (such as fruits) come from plants
3. Produce a product working with his peers

Objective: To plant seed, care for it, and watch it bear fruit

Materials: Purchased potting soil (or make it from soil, sphagnum moss and sand), large clay or plastic pots, ornamental pepper, cherry tomato, or gourd seeds, water

Procedure: If there are more than one child, work in groups of two children per planting pot.

1. Fill pot with soil.
2. With fingers, make a small hole in the center.
3. Place two or three seeds in the hole.
4. Cover with small amount of soil.
5. Water carefully.
6. Water as needed during growth.
7. When plants are about two inches tall, remove smaller one, leaving the strongest looking plant.
8. Let child look at plants as they bud, blossom and bear fruit.

Observing Progress: Did each child share and verbally interact with his partner during this activity?

Follow-up: Pick fruit from the plant, wash, cut in small pieces and have a tasting party. If squash was planted, remove the seeds and roast them, salt and eat.

sandbox counting

KEY: SM CN SP

Goals: Helping child to:
1. Understand concept of number (amount)
2. Engage in sensorimotor play

Objective: To make groups of molded sand "cups" to correspond with an amount or number given

Materials: Sandbox with sand, cups of various sizes, bucket of water with which to dampen sand

Procedure:
1. Allow child to free play first.
2. Demonstrate molding and unmolding cups of sand.
3. Ask child to mold one cup of sand and then unmold it. Child then does two cups, then three cups, and so on.
4. Talk casually with the child about size of the cups and amount of sand. Ask questions which encourage comparisons. Have child count how many cups of sand he has unmolded.

Observing Progress: Was child successful in unmolding?

Did child understand the concept of numbers involved? of comparisons?

Follow-up:
- Make a circle of unmolded sand cups. With a supply of buttons, poker chips or small balls, play a game to see how many chips each child can get in the center of his circle.
- Make a line of unmolded sand cups about a foot apart. Let child have fun "ringing" the sand cups with a ring cut out of styrofoam or one made of plastic or stout rope. Half the fun is knocking the piles of sand down.

63

sand castles

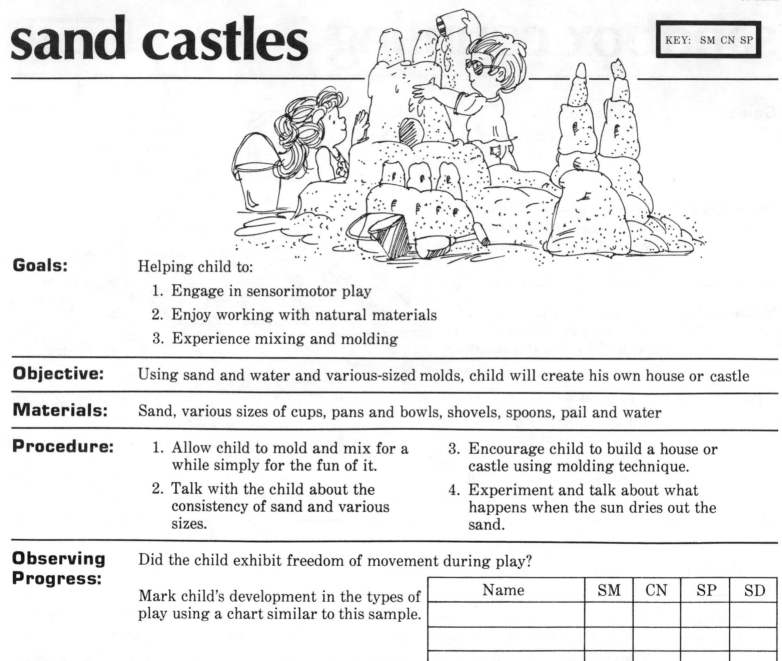

KEY: SM CN SP

Goals: Helping child to:

1. Engage in sensorimotor play
2. Enjoy working with natural materials
3. Experience mixing and molding

Objective: Using sand and water and various-sized molds, child will create his own house or castle

Materials: Sand, various sizes of cups, pans and bowls, shovels, spoons, pail and water

Procedure:

1. Allow child to mold and mix for a while simply for the fun of it.
2. Talk with the child about the consistency of sand and various sizes.
3. Encourage child to build a house or castle using molding technique.
4. Experiment and talk about what happens when the sun dries out the sand.

Observing Progress: Did the child exhibit freedom of movement during play?

Mark child's development in the types of play using a chart similar to this sample.

Name	SM	CN	SP	SD

Follow-up: Make mud pies and cakes to "sell".

modeling

Goals: Helping child to:

1. Develop eye/hand coordination
2. Enjoy sensory experiences
3. Build concepts of forms and shapes
4. Experience an emotional release

Objectives: Child will:

1. Work clay by beating and pounding, followed by breaking and rolling
2. Produce and name a product
3. Pull out or add details, such as nose, ears, arms, legs

Materials: Clay, sawdust and wheat paste, or salt ceramic, flour or water paste.

Procedure: You will:

1. Provide frequent opportunities so child can explore the material.
2. Encourage feeling, handling, and verbalizing.
3. Not model or show how to make something.
4. Keep materials soft and pliable by storing properly.

Observing Progress: Does the child become involved in the process of exploring and manipulating the clay? Is the child able to go beyond simple pounding to creating beginning products?

Follow-up: Provide as many experiences of working in clay as child needs to allow development from sensorimotor play to symbolic play.

65

clay zoo

Goals: Helping child to:
1. Develop small muscle skills by manipulating clay or play dough
2. Gain experience in a three-dimensional medium
3. Move from sensorimotor play into symbolic play

Objectives:
1. To create animals out of clay
2. To build cages in which to house animals

Materials: Clay or play dough (see page 144)

Procedure: Explain to child, "Today we are going to make a clay zoo."

Talk with the child about the animals at the zoo. (This is a good activity following a trip to the zoo.)

Option I Let child:
1. Work with the clay until it is warm and malleable.
2. Roll or pat out strips and balls.
3. Join together to form an animal of child's choice.

Option II
1. Mold animal out of one lump of clay.
2. Let dry.
3. Make cages from stick type building sets.
4. Put animals in cages.
5. Play zoo making animal sounds.

Observing Progress: Did the child create an animal? Did he role play? Did he move into symbolic play?

KEY: SM CN SP

Follow-up: Invite friends or parents to see the "zoo". Sing song "Look, Our Class Has Made a Zoo" to the tune of "Old MacDonald Had a Farm".

Look, Our Class Has Made a Zoo

Look, our class (or child's name) has made a zoo, ee-aye-ee-aye-oh.

And in this zoo we (he/she) have a bear (or any animal), ee-aye-ee-aye-oh.

"With a growl, growl here and a growl, growl there

"Here a growl, there a growl, everywhere a growl, growl

"Our whole class (or child's name) has made a zoo! ee-aye-ee-aye-oh!

pretend cookies

Goal: Helping child to:

Move from sensorimotor activity to construction to symbolic and/or sociodramatic play

Objective: To engage in symbolic and/or dramatic play through pretending to be a baker baking cookies

Materials: Clay, rolling pin, cookie sheet, large box, aprons, cookie cutters, real cookies

Procedure: Explain to the child:

1. *Let's play we are going to have a party and we need to make some cookies for the party. We can make our cookies from the play dough. This big box will be our stove. We can bake our cookies in it.*

2. *Bakers usually wear big aprons, so let's put our baking aprons on. There, now you look just like a baker.*

3. *I'll be your helper and roll out this little piece of dough with the rolling pin.* (Demonstrate.) *Okay, Mr. (Miss) Baker, it's time for you to get busy so that we have the cookies ready for the party.*

4. *Here is a cookie cutter, Mr. Baker. Would you like your helper to cut out one cookie?* (Demonstrate.) *I'll help you by putting the cookie on this cookie sheet. There! Is there anything you would like your helper to do?*

5. *Are these cookies all ready to be baked in the oven? Pop them in the oven then, Mr. Baker. I'll turn the heat up in the oven so the cookies will bake.* (Make motion of turning heat up.)

6. *Do you think the cookies are baked? Maybe we should peek in the oven and see if they are done. Are they done? Good, let's take them out. Say, they look good enough to eat! We are all ready for the party.*

7. *We can't really eat these play dough cookies, can we? No, these cookies would taste awful. They are made from play dough. But I have some real cookies. We can eat them at our party.*

Helpful Hints: It is important that you introduce the child to the ideas of baker and baking before you use this activity. Substitute props can be used instead of the real things. An empty bottle can be a rolling pin; a piece of heavy cardboard, a cookie sheet; and dish towels or pieces of sheet, baker's aprons. A large cardboard box makes a good stove. If you wish, cut an oven door in one side of the box, paint stove grills on the top and use the stove in other play cooking activities.

KEY: SM CN SP SD

Observing Progress: Was the child able to engage in:

symbolic play?   isolation play?   parallel play?   sociodramatic play?

Follow-up:
- Play baker and make a loaf of bread or rolls in a muffin pan from clay. Add a baker's hat to your props by turning over the open end of a paper bag several times to make a cuff which will fit the child's head.
- Share the poem "Baker".

Baker

I'd like to be a baker
With a white cap on my head,
And a big, shiny oven
Full of loaves of fragrant bread.

Best of all I'd bake some cookies—
Those that children like to eat,
And all my friends could come and munch
Eat crunchy, tasty treat.

I'd make delicious cupcakes—
Coconut or chocolate drop.
Lemon pies I'd learn to bake
With meringue spread on top.

—Jean Brabham McKinney

Reprinted from *Nursery Days*, June 15, 1969.
Copyright ©1969 by Graded Press.

Activity adapted from *Learning Activities for the Preschool Child*, by Rita Watrin, Paul A. Furfey. ©1978 by Litton Education Publishing, Inc.
Used by permission of D. Van Nostrand Company.

no-bake cookies

Goals: Helping child to:

1. Develop small muscle and eye/hand coordination
2. Develop and expand concepts of housekeeping tasks
3. Follow directions to make a product

Objectives:

1. To measure ingredients, cook and shape cookies
2. To wash dishes used in making cookies

Materials: Ingredients for recipe (see below), medium size saucepan, measuring cup, mixing bowl, wooden spoon, wax paper, stove or hot plate

Procedure:

Cocoa Balls	
½ c. milk	½ c. butter
2 c. sugar	3 c. oatmeal
6 T. cocoa	

You will:

1. Make a picture chart of ingredients to be used.
2. Allow child to measure ingredients as much as possible. Talk about texture, smell, taste of ingredients as they are added.
3. Place sugar, milk and butter in sauce pan.
4. Boil and stir for five minutes. Remove from heat.
5. Stir in oatmeal and cocoa. Cool until cool enough to handle.
6. Roll mixture into one-inch balls. Place on waxed paper.
7. Wash and dry utensils used in baking.
8. Enjoy eating the cookies.

Observing Progress: Did the child participate freely in the activity?
Was he able to follow directions and make product?

Follow-up:

Finger Gelatin

2 ½ cups water

1 (6 oz.) package gelatin mix—any flavor

2 packages unflavored gelatin

½ cup sugar

Dissolve unflavored gelatin in one cup of cold water. In a saucepan, bring 1 cup water to a boil and add gelatin mix and sugar. Stir and bring back to a boil. Remove from heat. Add gelatin mixture and ½ cup cold water. Pour into a greased pan. Refrigerate until firm. Using small shape cookie cutters, allow child to cut into shapes. Store leftovers in covered container in refrigerator. Eat and enjoy.

five finger puppets

KEY: SM CN SP SD

Goals: Helping child to:

1. Develop sensorimotor skills

2. Gain experience in manipulating clay or dough

3. Gain experience working in three-dimensional form

4. Move through sensorimotor play into symbolic and dramatic play

Objectives:

1. To construct finger puppets from play dough and miscellaneous items

2. To engage puppets in symbolic play, either in isolation, parallel play, or interacting with others

Materials: Purchase or make play dough (see page 144); small items, such as raisins, cereal, small marshmallows or stones; sticks; small pieces of fabric to use as eyes, nose, mouth and hats

Procedure: Child will:

1. Put blob of dough onto finger.

2. Mold dough into face shape covering finger.

3. Give face a personality by adding eyes, nose, mouth, and hat.

4. Make at least one other puppet.

5. Engage puppets in conversation. (You may need to encourage symbolic play by asking through a puppet of your own, questions which the child can answer, such as:

   My, you are certainly nice looking. What is your name? Mine is Bob. I am a firefighter. What do you do?)

6. Child can engage his own puppets in symbolic play or participate with another child. If the child does not wish to engage in this type of play, do not force him to do so.

Observing Progress: Was child able to use play dough in controlled, expressive construction?

Was he able to engage in symbolic play? In isolation play? In parallel play? With others? Imitative role play? Make-believe with objects for at least five minutes? Use language to maintain play?

clay puzzles

Goals: Helping child to:

1. Understand lines and shapes
2. Develop small muscle skills by manipulating clay

Objectives:

1. To construct a puzzle from clay
2. To match shapes with holes in clay

Materials: Clay, newspapers or plastic to cover floor or table, rolling pin, plastic or blunt knives

Procedures:

I
1. Work with clay until it is warm and malleable.
2. Divide into two- or three-inch balls.
3. Pound or roll out flat.
4. Cut or shape each piece so edges meet.

Or

II
1. Roll out clay.
2. Cut shape out of middle.
3. Remove shape and replace.
4. Cut as many shapes as interest and time allow.
5. Rework whenever necessary.

Observing Progress: Was child able to make a puzzle from clay?

Did he gain increased motor skill as he worked?

Follow-up: Allow child to use metal cookie cutters to cut shapes out of clay. Replace shapes.

sculptures

Goals: Helping child to:

1. Develop sensorimotor skills
2. Gain experience manipulating clay or play dough
3. Gain experience working in three-dimensional form

Objective: To make a sculpture from miscellaneous objects and play dough or clay

Materials: Clay or play dough (see page 144), wire, straw, sticks, yarn, and potatoes

Procedure: Child will:

1. Manipulate and form dough to make an object which can be used as a base for sculpture work.
2. Organize and affix objects of his own selection to create his own individual sculpture. You may wish to guide the child into a wire sculpture, a straw sculpture, a potato sculpture, or a menagerie sculpture.

Observing Progress: Did child use this medium in controlled, expressive construction?

Did he gain confidence as he worked?

Follow-up: Allow two or three children to work together on a larger sculpture. Encourage conversation and play.

bread kids

Goals: Helping child to:

1. Learn to follow directions
2. Gain experience manipulating dough
3. Have a direct sensory experience
4. Develop creativity

Objective: To shape a figure made from bread dough, bake it and eat it

Materials: Frozen bread dough (purchased from store or make your own), cookie sheets, shortening, raisins (optional), and oven

Procedure:

1. Follow recipe on package letting dough double or triple in size.
2. Punch down.
3. Give a workable amount to child.
4. Ask child to shape his own dough figure. He will need a body, head, two arms and two legs. Raisins may be added for eyes and buttons.
5. Place figure on greased cookie sheet. Cover with cloth.
6. Let double in size.
7. Bake at 375° for 20 to 40 minutes depending on size.

Observing Progress: Was the child successful in making a product in a controlled, expressive manner?

Follow-up: Make butter to spread on bread before eating. You will need one pint heavy cream, an egg beater, large bowl, slotted spoon. Pour cream into bowl. Beat with beater. Stop and taste when you reach the whipped cream stage. Continue beating until flecks of butter appear. Drain off the milk through the slotted spoon. Mash the butter together to make a ball. Taste. Add a little salt. It's ready to use on your "bread kids".

pasting, cutting and tearing

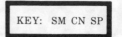

Goals: Helping child to:

1. Develop muscle control and eye/hand coordination
2. Experience self-expression and creative growth
3. Become aware of concepts of form and shape

Objectives: Child will:

1. Feel, manipulate, and explore using paste, scissors and paper for pasting, cutting and tearing
2. Develop control in using scissors
3. Combine colors and textures

Materials: Scissors, variety of colors and textures of paper, fabrics, and materials

Procedure:

1. Allow child to paste, cut and tear aimlessly, exploring the possibilities of the material.
2. Encourage skill development in controlling scissors and combining colors and textures.

Observing Progress: Is the child gradually experiencing more control and freedom in working with these materials?

Follow-up: Make a collage or montage related to the concept being studied or just to free form.

wet chalk

Goals: Helping child to:

1. Express himself through drawing
2. Learn control with wet chalk
3. Experiment with combining colors
4. Develop concepts of color, line and texture

Objective: To draw designs or pictures with wet chalk

Materials: Newspaper, art or construction paper, colored chalk, water in small plastic containers

Procedure:

1. Spread newspaper and provide child with drawing materials.
2. Have child dip chalk in water and then mark on paper.
3. Let child experiment with combining colors.

Observing Progress:

1. Was the child able to control the wet chalk?
2. Did the child combine colors?
3. Was the child mainly experimenting with the medium of wet chalk or did he move on to create a picture?

Follow-up: Spray with lacquer and mount picture on a construction paper frame. Display in room.

paper bag masks

KEY: CN SP

Goal:

Helping child to:

Better understand himself and others by understanding feelings

Objectives:

1. To recognize and name emotions (happy, sad, angry)
2. To verbally relate how he expresses feelings

Materials:

Large paper bag, scissors, crayons or felt-tip markers, paper cup, transparent tape, glue, small pieces of paper

Procedure:

Child will:

1. Put bag over his head. (You can carefully use a crayon to mark where eye holes should be.)
2. Cut out two holes for eyes.
3. Use crayons to draw face representing a particular emotion. (More than one mask can be made.)
4. Use paper cup for nose, paper strips for hair if desired.
5. Take some time to talk with the child about his feelings. (You might want to develop a "feelings" discussion before the construction of the masks.)

Discussion starters:

How can you tell if a person is happy? How do you act when you're happy? What makes you happy...sad...angry. Always accept what the child says. Acknowledge how he feels and then help him think of better ways to express what he's feeling. Example: Anger—child says he feels like hitting. Accept this and then say, "How else can you let someone know that you're angry?...Yes, you can tell the person and then tell him why, so he won't do it again."

Observing Progress:

Was the child able to verbalize different expressions of emotions?

Follow-up:

Using first the masks and then words, allow child to role play with another.

sew-on vest

Goals: Helping child to:

1. Develop a sense of pride in himself
2. Develop a sense of identity

Objective: To construct a vest (or use a premade one) and to apply decorations which are meaningful to the child

Materials: Vest (sewn or purchased), felt or iron-on fabric in a variety of colors, glue or needle and thread

Procedure:

1. Give child a vest either completed or with side seams unsewn.
2. Let child sew up vest with needle and thread or glue seems together
3. Child draws decorations of things that are special to him on pieces of fabric. (Examples: family members, memoirs, pets, and initials.)
4. Sew or glue fabric onto vest.
5. Wear.

Observing Progress: Is the child proud of his vest? Does he wear it? Did he talk with others about it?

Follow-up: Child can make an experience book related to the special things in the child's life.

crayon rubbing

KEY: SM CN

Goals: Helping child to:
1. Make designs
2. Develop small muscle coordination
3. Produce color with a crayon

Objective: To create a design on paper through the technique of crayon marking

Materials: Sandpaper, cardboard, leaves, lace doily, straw mat or anything child wishes to transfer onto paper, crayons—short length without paper coverings, 9″ x 12″ paper of any type

Procedure:
1. Keep material to be rubbed over in place by affixing it to desk or table-top with rubber cement. Let cement dry.
2. Have child place paper over item and using a side of the crayon, rub back and forth on the paper until an image appears. (More then one color can be used.)
3. To remove rubber cement from table, just rub it with fingers. It will brush right off. Do *not* use water to clean up.

Observing Progress: Is the child manipulating crayon in a controlled, effective manner?

Follow-up Use completed crayon rubbings as place mats. Cover with clear, plastic wrap or clear, self-adhesive acetate. Talk about the materials and colors that were used.

collage making

Goals: Helping child to:

1. Develop small motor skill
2. Be creative; use his imagination
3. Develop concept of texture, shape, design

Objective: To create a collage

Materials: White glue, brush for spreading glue, heavy paper or cardboard, small boxes full of odds and ends, such as papers (tissue and construction papers, wallpapers, newspapers, sandpaper, cards or magazine pictures with torn edges), fabrics, foods (macaroni, lentils, peas, beans), natural materials (leaves, weeds, bark, rocks, cotton, yarn), miscellaneous items (ribbons, foil, straws, toothpicks, and buttons)

Procedure:

1. Tell the children that *today, we are going to make 'bumpy pictures' called collages.*
2. Demonstrate how to apply glue and pieces of odds and ends.
3. Give each child a piece of paper and access to the boxes of materials.
4. Child selects his objects and glues them to the paper. Let each child work at his own speed.
5. Encourage child to fill up paper, but do not insist if he says he is finished.
6. Allow plenty of time for glue to dry.

Observing Progress: Did child understand process of making a collage?

Does he show progressive skill in sensorimotor activity?

Follow-up: If child is mature enough to clean up without supervision, leave collage materials out so that the child can work in his free time.

sidewalk drawing

Goals: Helping child to:

1. Express his emotions through drawing and movement

2. Develop large muscle coordination

3. Develop concepts of texture, color and line

Objective: To scribble or draw pictures or designs with chalk on sidewalk or paved playground

Materials: Concrete sidewalk or part of blacktop or concrete playground, white and colored chalk or rocks which are chalky

Procedure:

1. Explain to children the nature of the activity and that any drawing produced will be only temporary because rain and traffic will cause the drawing to disappear.

2. Child begins drawing at the top of work area so that picture does not become smeared.

3. Let child scribble or experiment with the chalk on concrete.

Observing Progress: Has child:

Drawn anything at all? Scribbled? Created with sense of design and form? Talked with others as he worked?

Follow-up:

- Draw a hopscotch on blacktop or cement outside. Let child practice hopping from one square to another.

- Draw a snail-shaped hopscotch. Let children jump from one space to the next.

chapter

Structured Materials Activities

Structured play materials include the following: carpentry, unit blocks, interlocking blocks, form boards, lotto, Montessori materials and puzzles. The child's use of these types of materials provides a basis for developing large and small muscle coordination and eye/hand coordination. These structured materials by their very nature provide a support for the child and help the child to develop inner controls. Through his interacting and working with structured materials the child develops concepts of size, shape, order, and number.

using tools

Goals: Helping child to:

1. Express aggressive impulses in an acceptable outlet
2. Develop eye/hand coordination and muscle control
3. Engage in problem solving
4. Become familiar with concepts of size and form

Objectives: Child will:

1. Handle and manipulate tools
2. Use tools for hammering, nailing and sawing
3. Make a product (may not be recognizable to adult)
4. Construct a recognizable object

Materials: Scraps of soft wood (flat and in a variety of shapes), nails, hammers, saws, screwdrivers, screws. Optional: tool board (pegboard), workbench, pliers, ruler, yardstick, hand drill, bits, dowel rods, clamps

Procedure:

1. Demonstrate the proper use of the tool.
2. Help child work with "real" tools.
3. Accept a product that satisfies the child.
4. Supervise the activity at all times.
5. Limit tools to the woodworking area.

Observing Progress: Has child used tools satisfactorily to:

- develop muscle (eye/hand) coordination through nailing, sawing, hammering?
- develop use of large muscles?
- as a means of emotional and physical release?
- grow socially through taking turns, working together, caring for tools?
- experiment?

Follow-up: Upon evaluation, encourage child to develop those areas he has not yet accomplished.

Foster symbolic play in the macrosphere by having two or more children work together.

Caution: This activity must be well supervised by an adult.

hammer the stump

Goals: Helping child to:

1. Develop sensorimotor skills
2. Develop eye/hand coordination
3. Release tensions and emotions

Objectives:

1. To learn the skills involved in hammering without having to make a product
2. To provide the practice needed to develop skill of hammering

Materials: Tree stump (or old railroad tie or very thick board), nails of various sizes (nails should be common wire and flat-headed), hammers

Procedure:

1. Start several nails in the stump so the child can begin hammering with less possibility of hitting his thumb and fingers.

2. Allow the child to pound at random, giving guidance and assistance when necessary.

Observing Progress: Keep a record of frequency with which child works at this type of activity.

Does he choose this activity as a method of relieving frustrations?

Follow-up: Make a Nail Name Board. Start nails (for an older child start only a few and mark where the rest should go) on board large enough to make child's name. Be sure nails are not too long—about three-fourths the length of the thickness of the board. The child will then be able to hammer nails into the board, thus spelling his own name.

Caution: Close supervision is required for the safe use of tools and nails.

nuts & bolts

Goals: Helping child to:

1. Develop small muscle coordination
2. Work with objects in the microsphere
3. Sort and classify on the basis of size, shape and texture

Objective: To separate a mixed pile of objects into separate classes—type, size, texture

Materials: Large jar with wide opening, egg carton, 4 to 5 each of plastic and rubber nuts, screws, bolts, and washers in several sizes. (Do not exceed more than 12 groupings.)

Procedure:

1. Fill the jar with all the objects.
2. Have child sort objects into the 12 compartments of the egg carton. (Child may work with another.)

   Sorting can be done by

   - type
   - size
   - texture

Observing Progress: Does the child exhibit confidence in manipulation? Did he work with another or alone?

Follow-up: Child can construct a "robot" using milk cartons, screws, bolts, nuts, and washers.

insect jars

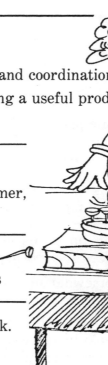

KEY: CN

Goals: Helping child to:
1. Develop small muscle control and coordination
2. Improve self-concept by making a useful product
3. Follow directions

Objectives:
1. To construct an insect jar
2. To develop skill in using hammer, nail and pounding block

Materials: Hammer, nails, pounding block, jar lid, jar, net for catching insects

Procedure:
1. Place jar lid on pounding block.
2. Using hammer and nail, pound holes in jar lid.
3. Attach lid to jar.
4. Use as insect jar.

Observing Progress: Was child able to construct a suitable product?

Follow-up: Using a net, the child can try to collect insects.

The insects, leaves, dirt and moisture can be placed in the jar for the child to observe.

Let insects go after observation.

build a boat to float

Goals: Helping child to:

1. Develop eye/hand coordination and muscle control
2. Follow directions to construct a product
3. Experience symbolic play and dramatic play

Objective: Using nails, hammer and wood scraps, child will construct a boat

Materials: Wood scraps of various sizes, hammer, flat-headed nails. Optional items can include white glue, toothpicks, scraps of fabric or paper.

Procedure:

1. Encourage child to build his own boat by nailing pieces of wood together.

   - Top should be somewhat smaller than the bottom piece.
   - Nails should have flat heads and be long enough to hold two pieces together without going completely through the wood.

2. The child may wish to put a flag on top by gluing a toothpick and paper or fabric scrap to the side of the top piece of wood.

3. Boat can be decorated using tempera paints or crayons.

Observing Progress: Was the child successful in completing the product?

Does he exhibit confidence in working with this medium?

Follow-up: Provide a tub or use a sink full of water where child can sail his boat. Symbolic and dramatic play can be encouraged by letting two or more children sail their boats together.

Caution: Close supervision is required for the safe use of tools and nails.

wire art

Goals: Helping child to:
1. Develop eye/hand and small muscle coordination
2. Follow directions
3. Construct a product

Objective: To construct an abstract or recognizable sculpture made of wire

Materials: Staple gun and staples, hammer, plastic coated electrician's wire of bright colors and scrap pieces of wood. (Use pipe cleaners and a school stapler with youngest children.)

Procedure:
1. Encourage child to manipulate a small piece of wire, 12-18 inches in length.
2. Ask him to make a design with the wire. Give additional pieces, if desired.
3. Assist child in attaching finished sculpture to wood block by stapling.
4. Allow each child time to tell about his sculpture.

Observing Progress: Was the child able to finish his sculpture? Was he able to verbalize about it?

Follow-up: Construct small group sculptures from empty boxes, all sizes and shapes. Glue together. Child can paint finished sculpture.

Caution: Close supervision is required for the safe use of wire and tools.

rubber band stretch

Goals: Helping child to:

1. Work comfortably in a structured activity
2. Develop fine motor skills
3. Develop concept of line and patterning
4. Develop perceptural motor skill

Objective: To make patterns by stretching rubber bands over nail heads hammered into wood

Materials: Any size or shape piece of wood, nails, hammer, colored rubber bands

Procedure: This activity can be done alone or in a small group. Use a small piece of wood for one child, a large board for a small group.

1. Hammer nails randomly over the board.

2. Stretch rubber bands on the nails thereby making various patterns and designs.

Observing Progress: Could the child hammer nails in board? Could the child create designs using the rubber bands? Did he talk about what he was doing?

Follow-up: Premade sets of boards in which nails are arranged in a pattern, such as a circle, square, triangle, or grid, can be used to help teach geometric shapes.

scrap wood sculpture

KEY: SM CN

Goals: Helping child to:

1. Develop eye/hand coordination and muscle control
2. Develop concepts of size, shape and form
3. Increase his interaction with others

Objective: To make a sculpture from pieces of wood

Materials: Small scrap pieces of wood (from lumberyard), heavy pieces of cardboard for use as bases, white glue

Procedure: This activity may be an individual or a small group activity.

1. Encourage children to experiment with pieces of wood, creating their own form.
2. Demonstrate how to glue pieces onto cardboard and other wood pieces.
3. Allow children to work together at their own speed.

Observing Progress: Was child able to create expressively?

Was he able to develop a sense of design and form?

Did he work alone?　with others?

Follow-up: Play the game, "Guess What Shape?"

Hold up a block having a specific shape (square, retangle, or triangle). Child scrambles through a large pile of blocks to find one which matches the one you're holding.

block play

Goals: Helping child to:

1. Have opportunities for isolated, parallel, and cooperative play
2. Gain sense of power and achievement in the physical world
3. Experience emotional release through dramatic play
4. Engage in physical experiences through lifting, carrying, and piling
5. Cultivate creative expression and a sense of design
6. Develop skills in problem solving, number concepts and language

Objectives: The child will:

1. Play with single blocks
2. Stack blocks, knock them down and stack them again
3. Create and name buildings
4. Distinguish between different types of buildings
5. Participate in dramatic play using block structures as props

Materials: Cardboard blocks which are hollow and large enough to make structures that the child can actually use

Procedure:

1. Provide enough space and materials.
2. Allow child to leave structure up when possible. Let child know when its time for cleanup.
3. Watch for ways of helping the passive child participate. Offer help when needed.

Observing Progress: Has the child used blocks satisfactorily to:

- Progress from SM to CN to SP to SD?
- Develop muscle coordination through lifting, carrying and piling?
- Create expressively and develop a sense of design and form?

- Exhibit cognitive growth through the development of concepts and language skills?
- Assist in the development of concepts of size, shape and language opportunities?
- Assist in the development of concepts of size, shape and number values.

Follow-up: Blocks can be used as a perfect resource for group learning times. Use them to demonstrate the concepts of shape, number, size, same and different.

junk city

Goals: Helping child to:

1. Develop creativity
2. Develop a concept of a city
3. Provide opportunity to interact with others

Objective: To create a sculpture out of junk items

Materials: Various sized boxes and cardboard rolls, clothespins, crayons

Procedure: Child will:

1. Construct miniature city or town.
2. Decorate with crayons or paint (if desired).
3. Populate with clothespin people.
4. Talk about what he has built.

Observing Progress: How long did the child work at the activity?   Did he work alone or with others?
Was verbal interaction occuring during construction?

Follow-up: Share *The Skyscraper* by Y. Liang (J.B. Lippincott, 1958) with the class. Let the children examine the pictures. Teach the singing game, "Round the Village" (From the *Golden Song Book*, Golden Press, 1964), updating it to say, "Round the City".

my little house

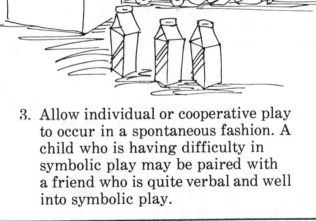

Goals: Helping child to:

: 1. Develop increased concept of home and housekeeping
2. Engage in symbolic and/or dramatic play

Objectives:
1. To construct a small house
2. To play house either in cooperation with others or in solitary play

Materials: Large wooden blocks, milk crates or boxes which have been taped shut, blanket or sheet, furnishings—pillows, doll beds, dolls, toys, cars and trucks.

Procedure:
1. Read to child *The Little House* by Virginia Lee Burton (Houghton & Mifflin) (see Bibliography).
2. Encourage child to construct his own house using the above mentioned items.
3. Allow individual or cooperative play to occur in a spontaneous fashion. A child who is having difficulty in symbolic play may be paired with a friend who is quite verbal and well into symbolic play.

Observing Progress: Keep weekly records of types and duration of symbolic play in which child participates.

Follow-up: Encourage child to draw, paint, or model in clay a representation of his own house.

railroad train

Goals: Helping child to:

1. Move from sensorimotor play to symbolic and dramatic play
2. Develop language skills as he speaks, listens and communicates
3. Build concepts of transportation and money

Objective: To role play railroad train with peers

Materials: Cardboard boxes at least two feet long, paper punch, paper tickets, triangle or bell, whistle, shakers or maracas

Procedure: Share book or books about trains before beginning activity (see Bibliography).

1. Line cardboard boxes up one behind the other, calling the front one the engine and the others passenger cars. Have one box for each child. One child can play engineer, one child can be given a triangle, bell or horn to signal the start of the train, another can make wheel sounds, and so on. Pieces of paper can be distributed as tickets and then collected by a conductor.
2. For younger children, individual play with a toy train might be needed before the above activity is initiated.

Observing Progress: Was the child able to:

Role play with objects? Maintain play for five minutes or more? Interact with peers? Use language to maintain play?

Follow-up: Promote sociodramatic play still further by making airplanes of two strips of wood (popsickle sticks) glued together. Make an airport from cardboard boxes. A piece of brown paper can be used as the landing strip. Boxes can be used as hangars, tunnel, terminal and tower.

shape sorter

Goals: Helping child to:

1. Sort blocks into groups with same shape
2. Match shapes with corresponding holes
3. Develop sensorimotor skill and eye/hand coordination

Objective:

1. To group blocks into piles having same shape
2. To match shapes with holes in sorting box

Materials: Premade shape sorter and several sets of blocks or shapes

Procedure:

1. Review shapes to be used with children. In addition to circle, triangle, and square, more advanced children can also use rectangle, oval and various other shapes.
2. Using only six blocks, ask child to group the blocks into piles of the same shape.
3. Demonstrate how to use shape sorter.
4. Using the circle shape only, allow child to find the proper hole and drop shape into it.
5. Gradually add more blocks, asking child to group like shapes together. Give as little help as possible, but do not allow child to become frustrated.

Observing Progress: Does the child exhibit cognitive growth through development of concepts related to shapes?

Did the child engage in solitary play? in parallel play? Did he verbalize during play?

Follow-up: With heavy paper and one of each shape, outline each shape with pencil or crayon. (This may be done by you or with the child.) Mix up the blocks and ask the child to place each block within its proper outline.

Activity adapted from *Learning Activities for the Preschool Child*, by Rita Watrin, Paul A. Furfey. ©1978 by Litton Education Publishing, Inc. Used by permission of D. Van Nostrand Company.

make a staircase

Goals: Helping child to:

1. Develop the concept of ordering
2. Move from sensorimotor play into symbolic play

Objectives:

1. To place blocks in order from shortest to tallest
2. To make a product (in this case a staircase) which can be used in symbolic and/or dramatic play

Materials: Varied sizes of rectangular blocks

Procedure:

1. Allow child time to play with blocks—to stack them, knock them down, and build them up again.

2. Ask child to order blocks from shortest to tallest; in other words, to make them into a staircase.

3. Ask child to make another staircase backing up to the first one (or children can work in pairs and make their staircases back to back).

4. Ask child to pretend his fingers are frogs and to jump his frogs up one end of the staircase and then down the other end.

5. Allow child to engage in construction and/or symbolic play as long as his interest allows.

Observing Progress: Was the child able to move from sensorimotor into symbolic or dramatic play?

Follow-up: Encourage the child to build other products, such as towers, garages, houses, fire stations.

interlocking milk cartons | KEY: SM SP |

Goal: Helping child to:

Move from sensorimotor play to symbolic play

Objective: To engage in sensorimotor play using homemade interlocking blocks

Materials: A number of quart milk cartons, well rinsed. You should cut a square the size of the bottom of the milk carton out of the side. Do this for each carton. (A paper cutting knife works well.) The cutout portion may be anywhere on the side of the carton. Stand cartons inside one another.

Procedure:
1. Demonstrate to child how cartons fit together.
2. Allow him on his own to build towers, buildings or sculptures of various kinds. Play with him helping him move from a sensorimotor activity to symbolic play, or pair him with another child if appropriate.

Observing Progress: What is the frequency of the child's play? Is he able to use it to move from sensorimotor play into symbolic play?

Follow-up: Make a garage out of milk carton blocks. Introduce small cars and trucks for symbolic play and dramatic play involvement.

treasure chest

KEY: SM SP SD

Goals: Helping child to:

1. Develop interest in adventuring
2. Develop sensorimotor, symbolic and sociodramatic play

Objectives:

1. To discover new playthings by unlocking secret treasure chest
2. To engage in sensorimotor, symbolic and/or dramatic play through the use of discovered treasure

Materials: Old trunk or wooden box with a lid or door to which hinges and hasp have been added, a lock and key

Procedure:

1. Build excitement by telling the child a locked treasure chest has been discovered. A note has been found stating that the chest contains some exciting things to do. (Have inside the chest a quantity of interlocking block systems to involve child in constructing and creating.)
2. Supply the child with the key to unlock the chest.
3. Encourage him to play with blocks on his own or to follow directions to make a specific product.

Observing Progress: What kinds of play did the child engage in? Sensorimotor in the microsphere? Symbolic play in isolation? in parallel play? Sociodramatic play with others? For at least 5 minutes? With a product?

Follow-up: The chest can be used to foster symbolic and sociodramatic play by changing its contents occasionally. Contents might be such things as puppets, telephones, pictures for montage making, dominoes, play money, or a magnet and magnetic tools. Guessing games can be played—what's inside the chest? Example, "It's made of metal. It's shaped like a horseshoe. It's red and grey and picks up things." Answer: "It's a magnet."

log cabin

KEY: SM CN SP SD

Goals: Helping child to:

1. Develop small muscle coordination
2. Progress from sensorimotor play to symbolic and/or sociodramatic play

Objective: To construct a log cabin from American or Lincoln logs

Materials: American or Lincoln logs

Procedure:

1. Talk with child about the nature and use of a log cabin.
2. Explain that it is a house built from logs.
3. Encourage child to build his own log cabin or to work with another child.

Observing Progress:

Did the child achieve the construction of a product?

Did he work alone?
with another?

Follow-up: Discuss types of houses and what they are made of. The child might want to make a house using play dough or clay or draw and paint a house.

build a city

Goals: Helping child to:

1. Move from sensorimotor play to symbolic play and sociodramatic play

2. Develop creative expression and a sense of design

3. Develop a concept of community

Objective: To build a city block after a model in the child's own experience

Materials: An assortment of interlocking blocks

Procedure:
1. You might enjoy taking your child on a field trip around your area. Discuss the types of buildings and how buildings and houses are laid out between streets.

2. Suggest, "Let's build a city with our blocks, today."

3. Ask each child or group of two to make a square for his/her or their block.

4. Have child put blocks (buildings) close enough together to form streets. Talk about houses and buildings on the block. (A good block to talk about might be the block immediately surrounding the school or other familiar structure.

   The play can take many directions. Child may wish to add cars and trucks, or a fire station with equipment, or a hospital or school. Encourage the child to verbalize and engage in symbolic and/or sociodramatic play.

Observing Progress: Did the child construct his own block?   Did he engage in symbolic play? in sociodramatic play?

Follow-up: Read *Wake Up City* by A. Tresselt (Lothrop, Lee and Shepherd, 1957). Discuss all the people who wake up in the city. Take a field trip around the block (if you are located in the city) or to the nearest downtown section.

robot

KEY: SM CN SP SD

Goals:	Helping child to:

1. Move from sensorimotor play to symbolic play
2. Develop language ability

Objective:

1. To construct a robot using interlocking blocks
2. To engage in a symbolic play activity with the robot as a prop

Materials: A variety of interlocking blocks

Procedure:

1. Talk about a robot with the child. What is a robot?

2. Suggest, "Let's make a robot out of our blocks today."

3. Encourage child to begin building a robot. Talk about relationship of parts as each piece is added.

4. Engage child or children in symbolic play with their robots.
Ask: "What is your robot's name?" "What does it do?" "Listen to how my robot, TuBeep, can talk. *'Beep, beep'*, let's move this block."

Observing Progress: Was the child able to move into symbolic play?

Follow-up: Child can construct another personality of his choice or perhaps an object such as a fire truck or a police car to be used in symbolic and/or sociodramatic play.

pegboards & pegs

KEY: SM

Goals: Helping child to:

1. Develop small motor coordination
2. Develop concepts of line and number
3. Develop perceptual motor skills

Objective: To create a pegboard pattern of one's own or one which duplicates that made by another person

Materials: Commercial pegboards and pegs, or boards made from acoustical tiles with golf tees for pegs or wood bases with holes drilled for insertion of pieces of ½ or ¼-inch dowels

Procedure: Allow any of the following types of play:

1. Random play where child makes his own design or pattern.
2. Pattern copy where you make a simple pattern on the chalkboard which the child tries to duplicate on his pegboard.
3. After pegs are inserted child can stretch rubber bands from one peg to another.

Observing Progress: Was the child able to duplicate patterns?

Did child work efficiently at a structured activity?

Follow-up: Lace shoe strings or plastic lacing through pegboard to form various designs.

string matchup

Goals: Helping child to:

1. Develop small muscle coordination
2. Learn to play with structured activity
3. Understand concept of number

Objective: To complete string matchup card by matching numeral to corresponding number of items and lacing string through proper holes to show understanding

Materials: Purchase or make a game similar to one shown.

Procedure:

1. The child matches the numeral on the left to the correct number of objects on the right. (You might need to demonstrate as the child may not know *right* from *left*.)

2. Thread the string through the hole of the correct number of dots or picture symbols for the number. (Demonstrate how threading should be done.)

   Note: A self-check answer sheet of the same size may be used after the child is finished, or he may choose a friend with whom he can check his responses.

Observing Progress: Did the child string the card properly? Was he comfortable with this structured activity?

Follow-up: Practice lacing (not tying) a wooden shoe (available at many toystores) or an adult's shoe. Be sure eyelets and laces are large enough for the child to work with comfortably.

sewing cards

Goals: Helping child to:

1. Develop small muscle coordination
2. Develop eye/hand coordination
3. Experience interaction with others

Objective: To complete the outlines of an object by threading yarn back and forth

Materials: Large, blunt needle, such as a rug or tapestry needle; sewing cards, either purchased or made; yarn or colored heavy thread or cord

Procedure:

1. Child threads needle. (You may need to help.)
2. Push needle in and out on the heavy, black dots. The long stitches go on the front side; the short stitches on the back.
3. Allow child to work slowly and carefully.

Observing Progress:

Was the child able to follow directions?

Was his product recognizable?

Follow-up: Allow child to tell something about the picture he has just completed or play Twenty Questions and have others try to guess what his card represents.

For example: "Do we wear it?"

"Is it good to eat?"

"Is it cooked on the stove?"

"Is it a vegetable?"

form puzzles

KEY: SM

Goals: Helping child to:

1. Develop small motor skills and perceptual motor skills
2. Develop attention span
3. Develop concept of two-dimensional form

Objective: To fit individual pieces of forms into the proper holes of the form boards

Materials: Form boards—either purchased or homemade. Form boards are a special type of puzzle into which individual forms are fitted. In the use of form boards, as well as of puzzles, there must be a range of difficulty so that every child can find puzzles which are challenging, not too easy and not too hard. The difficulty is determined by the number of pieces and the way in which the pieces are cut.

Procedure:

1. Allow the child to work choosing his own level.
2. If he becomes frustrated, choose an easier board.
3. If he finishes always with ease, suggest or bring for him a more difficult board.

Observing Progress: Was the child easily frustrated? bored?

Was he able to find his own level of difficulty?

Follow-up: Let the child make his own puzzle by gluing a picture onto thin cardboard. When dry, let him cut the picture into several pieces and share with a friend, putting it back together. Store the pieces in an envelope.

picture card puzzles

Goals:

Helping child to:

1. Develop small muscle coordination
2. Develop communication skills
3. Learn to play with structured activities

Objectives:

1. To put together the puzzle, relating activity with the objects used in that activity
2. To verbalize the relationship of objects to activity

Materials:

Make or purchase puzzles of activities and objects related to the activities, such as car and driving, books and reading, apron and cooking, swimsuit and swimming.

Procedure:

1. Help child identify the objects in the pictures.
2. Have child explain why the pictures go together. For example, a needle and sewing go together because you use a needle when you sew.

Observing Progress:

Did the child put the puzzles together properly?   Was he able to tell why?

Was he comfortable working with a structured activity?

Follow-up:

Encourage the child or a group of children to act out roles represented by the activities or objects on the puzzles.

shapes lotto

KEY: SM

Goals: Helping child to:

1. Develop the concepts of shapes
2. Learn to take turns
3. Engage in a structured form of play

Objective: To play a shapes game using a set of rules

Materials: Purchased shape lotto game or homemade game. (See page 144.)

Procedure:

1. In turn, each player draws a card from a pile and places it on his game card covering the shape which matches that on his card.
2. If the card does not match an empty space, the player places it face down in a separate pile.
3. Play continues until all spaces are covered.

Observing Progress: Was the child successful in completing the activity?

Was he able to play in a controlled, orderly manner?

Follow-up: Use the same type game, but with numbers instead of shapes.

lotto fun

Goals: Helping child to:

1. Develop sensorimotor skills through a moderately structured activity
2. Develop visual perception and discrimination skills
3. Interact with others

Objective: Following your directions, child will play lotto games with you or other children

Materials: Two sets of homemade or commercial lotto games having identical pictures

Procedure: Various methods of using lottos:

A. 1. Give each child a lotto board.
   2. You keep all the cards. Hold up one at a time.
   3. Ask child to point to the identical picture on his board.
   4. If correct, give him the card to place over his picture.
   5. If not correct, aid him in finding the correct picture.

B. 1. Say the name of the picture.
   2. The child points to it on the board.
   3. Give the child the card to place over his picture.

C. 1. Describe the picture without showing or naming it.
   2. The child points to it on the board.
   3. Give the card to the child to place over his picture.

D. 1. The child describes a picture on his board.
   2. You give him the card which matches his description.
   3. Child places it over his picture.

E. 1. One child or a pair of children have a gameboard and one set of cards.
   2. One at a time, each child matches cards to pictures on the board.

Observing Progress: Is this activity used as a change of pace for more active play?

Is it a frequent choice made by the child?

Follow-up: Construct your own lotto games using colors, shapes, pictures, and numbers.
Make a large gameboard with four to six pictures on the board. Construct matching individual picture cards.

jingle lotto

Goals: Helping child to:

1. Develop concepts of shape, size, number and color

2. Develop visual perception skills

3. Develop sensorimotor skills in a structured activity

Objective: To play a game of matching in response to a jingle

Jingle

What have we here?

What do you see?

Find the one that matches

And bring it to me!

Materials: Two sets of cards with either shapes, numerals, colors, or pictures on them

Procedure:
1. Hand out one set of cards to child or a small group of children. (You keep one set.)
2. Hold up one shape and say the jingle.
3. Child gives you the matching card.

Observing Progress: Did the child engage in controlled sensorimotor activity?

Did he display a reasonable amount of confidence?

Follow-up: A more complicated game would be to use two or more variables, such as color and size together or color, shape and size.

paper punch dominoes

KEY: SM

Goals: Helping child to:
1. Develop the concept of number
2. Develop sensorimotor skills
3. Increase his perceptual skills

Objectives:
1. To match a set of domino cards
2. To match dots and build with cards

Materials: Unlined, three-by-five-inch index cards, paper punch

Procedure:
1. Prepare cards for numerals 0 through 6 (0-6) in advance by drawing a line down the center of each card. (The number of cards depends on the age and development of the child.)
2. Mark dots on each half to indicate where the child is to punch holes.
3. The child punches out holes on the cards. (If hole punches are not available, gummed circles or stars can be placed over the dots.)

4. Child uses his set of cards by matching like ends.
5. Two children each can prepare a set and play together, taking turns matching like numbers.

Observing Progress: Was the child able to engage successfully in a controlled sensorimotor activity?

Follow-up:
- Share counting books, such as *Count and See* by T. Hoban, and *Numbers of Things* by H. Oxenbury.
- Sing counting songs, such as "Ten Little Indians" and "This Old Man".

a b c lotto

Goals:	Helping child to: 1. Develop visual perception 2. Develop sensorimotor skill in a structured activity
Objective:	To match each cutout letter with an identical letter on paper
Materials:	Alphabet letters—cut out, a large sheet of paper divided into twenty-six sections with a letter printed in each square (letters may be either in order or mixed up)
Procedure:	The child will cover each square on the paper with a card having the same letter.
Observing Progress:	Was the child able to match letters? Did the child work in isolation? in parallel play? in cooperation with others?
Follow-up:	Cut out letters from sandpaper. Have a touch guessing game with eyes closed to see if child can tell by feel what letter he is touching.

blindfold guess

Goals: Helping child to:

1. Develop tactile awareness
2. Develop cognitive ability in distinguishing similarities and differences
3. Develop small muscle control

Objective: To match pieces of fabric according to their texture

Materials: Blindfold, pairs of fabric with different textures (fabrics should be cut in equal sized squares), box

Procedure:

1. Blindfold child. (Child can keep eyes closed if blindfolding presents a problem.)
2. Dump box of fabrics onto tabletop. (With younger children, you may want to begin this activity using only three or four types of fabric.)
3. Child finds two pieces of fabric which feel the same.

4. Ask the child to tell you how each square feels. (You may have to tell the child how it feels to you.)

Observing Progress: Was the child able to match like pieces of fabric?

Was he able to work in a controlled, orderly manner?

Follow-up: Put one set of squares into a paper bag. Place it on the floor. Arrange a matching set side by side on the floor. Have the child reach into the bag and feel one of the fabric squares. Without looking at it or pulling it out, have him point to the one on the floor which he thinks he is feeling in the bag. Allow him to check to see if it matches. Continue until all the pieces are matched.

geometric solids

KEY: SM

Goals: Helping child to:

1. Develop sense of touch
2. Develop small muscle skills
3. Develop cognitive ability to compare and distinguish

Objective: To feel and group like geometric solids while blindfolded

Materials: Blindfold, geometric solids—two sets of a cube, cylinder, rectangle, oval, circle, and triangle

Procedure:

1. Beginning with two pairs of solids, the child will touch and handle each. You may wish to help the child by explaining what to look for and how to touch in order to distinguish and compare.
2. Blindfold child.
3. The child will touch each solid and place like pairs on the table.

Observing Progress: Was the child able to group like pairs together?

Was he able to work in a controlled, orderly manner?

Follow-up: Use constructive triangles to build geometrical shapes—good for eye/hand coordination skill development.

typewriter fun

Goals: Helping child to:

1. Develop small muscle coordination
2. Develop visual perception skills
3. Develop concept of letters

Objective: To strike one key at a time on a typewriter making symbols appear on paper

Materials: Discarded typewriter, 8 ½" x 11" paper or newsprint

Procedure: The child uses the typewriter to:

1. Learn names of letters and numbers.
2. Experience the pleasure of seeing something appear on paper when the key is pushed.
3. Copy something (such as his own name which has been previously typed).

Note: Stress the rule of hitting one key at a time. Many children may be interested only in the motor aspects. Do not force attention to letters, but be aware of the child who may be ready for them.

With younger children, you may need to be nearby to help roll in paper and cope with sticking keys. With older children, the typewriter may be available for use at any time when noise is not a problem.

Observing Progress: Was the child involved in motor activity only? Was the child involved in learning letters and/or copying letters or words?

Follow-up: The child may type a word of his choice which you have written or typed for him to copy. He then may elaborate by crayoning or drawing a picture on the same paper.

knobbed cylinders

Goals: Helping child to:

1. Develop sensorimotor control and coordination
2. Develop cognitive ability in observing and distinguishing
3. Develop small muscle control in hands as he grasps knobs

Objective: To fit the knobbed cylinders into proper places while blindfolded

Materials: Knobbed cylinders and cylinder form board, blindfold

Procedure:

1. Allow child to fit the cylinders into the proper place without the use of a blindfold.
2. Show him how to distinguish size and shape of cylinders and recesses by exploring with his fingers.
3. Blindfold the child.
4. Repeat the above procedure following steps 1 through 2.

Observing Progress: Did the child's skill increase with continued practice and manipulation?

Follow-up: Use a graduated tower with pieces that increase in dimension. Child builds the tower, developing tactile discrimination. Use this activity with or without the blindfold.

graduated cylinders

Goals: Helping child to:

1. Develop small muscle coordination
2. Develop control in structured activity
3. Learn how to perform an exercise
4. Learn by repetition and discover how to correct himself

Objective: To manipulate and stack cylinders one on top of the other in correct order of graduation

Materials: Colored knobless cylinders of graduated sizes. (These cylinders correspond in dimension to the knobbed cylinders, on page 118.)

Procedure:

1. The child builds with the cylinders, gradually developing muscle coordination.
2. Allow the inexperienced child to work beside or near one who has previously been successful in finding the proper place for each cylinder.
   The inexperienced child will soon see how it is done and learn by trial and error.

Observing Progress: Was the child able to perform the exercise?

Did he correct himself?

Follow-up: Use cube people. Child learns the positions which allow blocks to fit together to make a cube thereby developing small muscle coordination and cognitive ability.

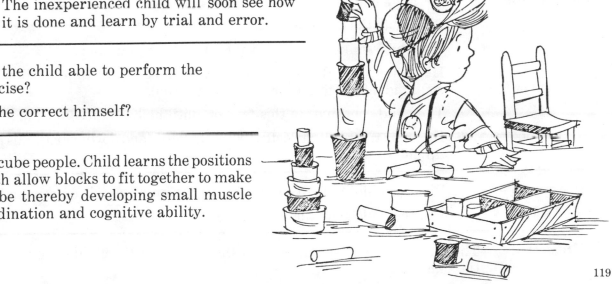

play me a tune

KEY: SM

Goals:

Helping child to:

1. Develop listening skills
2. Perform the exercise of pairing like sounds
3. Learn musical tunes which he can repeat
4. Learn to control motor impulses

Objectives:

1. To find bell with sound identical to first bell struck.
2. To learn the order of sounds in the musical scale (major)

Materials:

Bells—two sets of a series of corresponding bells (one set should be movable), a small hammer

Procedure:

1. Arrange one set of bells with tones do, re, mi, fa, sol, la, ti, do.
2. Scramble the other set of bells.
3. The child strikes the first bell (do) with the hammer.
4. He then strikes the set of scrambled bells one at a time until he finds one which has a sound identical to the first one struck (do).
5. The child continues in this fashion until he has paired all the tones.
6. He then strikes all the notes (bells) upwards and downwards thus hearing the entire scale up and down.

Observing Progress:

1. Was the child able to control his motor impulses, sit quietly and listen to the tones?
2. Did the child pair the tones correctly?

Follow-up:

The piano may be used in place of the bells after the child develops some skills in hearing the tones.

number puzzles

Goals: Helping child to:

1. Develop eye/hand coordination
2. Recognize that parts put together make a whole
3. Work on a structured activity in a controlled manner

Objectives:

1. To match the concept of number with numeral and matching visual representation
2. To piece together two puzzle pieces to make a whole

Materials: A set of ten, two-piece puzzles—one half showing the numeral; the other half a picture of items corresponding to the number

Procedure:

1. Discuss numbers one through ten.
2. Play guessing games with puzzles. Try the following: "Can you find the numeral 5?" "Bring it to me." / "Can you find a picture with five things on it?" / "Let's see if you can fit these two together." / "Look, you've made a complete puzzle."
3. Allow the child to work with the number puzzles, giving assistance when necessary.

Observing Progress: Was the child able to complete the activity successfully in a controlled manner?

Follow-up: Use the same type of puzzle, but with words or pictures which relate to a unit or area of study rather than numbers (baker and bread, firefighter and fire hat, and so on).

smile face puzzles

Goals: Helping child to:

1. Begin problem solving
2. Develop eye/hand coordination
3. Work on a structured activity in a controlled manner

Objectives:

1. To replace each puzzle piece correctly
2. To recognize positional relationships among puzzle pieces

Sample

Materials: Paper plates, glue, pieces for mouth, nose and eyes

Procedure:

1. Press paper plate flat.
2. Make a happy face by gluing eyes, nose and mouth to plate. Let dry. (Face can be made with crayons or markers, if preferred.)
3. Cut the plate apart as the dashed lines in sample indicate.

4. Talk about the puzzle with the child. Ask him to point out Smile Face's eyes, nose and mouth. Play peek-a-boo type games with missing pieces.

Note: In the autumn, make a jack-o'-lantern face; in February, a Valentine smile face.

Observing Progress: Was the child successful in completing the activity?

Did he work in a controlled but uninhibited manner? Did he verbalize or converse during his work?

Follow-up: Child can draw or paste other pictures on a paper plate. Cut into three pieces. Put them together. Store them in an envelope and share with a friend.

magazine puzzles

Goals: Helping child to:
1. Fit parts to the whole
2. Develop eye/hand coordination

Objective: To take apart and reconstruct the puzzle pieces of a familiar object

Materials: Large magazine pictures (simple for younger child; more complex for older child), cardboard, glue

Procedure:
1. Choose one large magazine picture for each child and paste it on cardboard.
2. Cut the picture into 4 or 5 pieces.
3. Child puts the puzzle together.

   Note: For less advanced children provide a complete duplicate of the puzzle picture so that the child can match the pieces to the complete picture.

Observing Progress: Was the child able to reconstruct the parts to make the whole picture?

Follow-up: Have children exchange puzzles with other children and put them together.

inset puzzles

Goals: Helping child to:

1. Recognize that parts put together make a whole
2. Experience problem solving
3. Develop eye/hand coordination skills

Objective:

1. To recognize shapes, colors and sizes
2. To become aware of positional relationships among objects and parts of objects
3. To learn the parts of an object, such as a person has arms, legs, head, hands, feet; a dog has a tail, head, ears and legs.
4. To take apart, manipulate and reconstruct a given puzzle

Materials: Purchased or homemade puzzles

Types of puzzles:

1. Three- and four-piece inset puzzles in which whole form or puzzle piece fits into a hole.
2. Simple homemade puzzles in which a picture is pasted onto a piece of cardboard and then cut into halves, thirds, or quarters.
3. Puzzles with more pieces that are cut around actual forms, such as most commercial wooden puzzles.
4. Jigsaw puzzles with pieces that have no relationship with the picture.

Procedure: If you are working with a young child:

1. Use puzzles that are simple, whole-object puzzles in which a puzzle piece represents a complete object—a ball, a clown, a shoe. Large wooden puzzles with colorful pieces are especially good. Remember, working with puzzles should be fun as well as a learning experience.
2. Offer verbal directions first. If needed, supply more direct manipulative help.

With older children:

1. Present puzzles first as whole picture. Verbally identify parts and relationships.

2. Demonstrate removing one piece. Name it and describe it.

3. Replace piece.

4. Have child try on his own. Give help as needed—talk about clues as to where pieces go (shape, relationship, color).

Observing Progress: Was the child experiencing an enjoyable game?   Did he reach his frustration level?

Follow-up: Allow the child to repeatedly do a puzzle he likes as it offers a fun source of reinforcement.

geometric shape puzzle

KEY: SM

Goals: Helping child to:

1. Recognize shapes, colors and sizes
2. Experience problem solving
3. Develop eye/hand coordination skills

Objective: To take apart and put a puzzle back together

Materials: Colored rubber puzzles of different shapes, such as triangles, circles and squares. For older children, each large shape may be filled with smaller shapes that fit tightly inside one another.

Procedure: The child will take puzzles apart, sort pieces, and fit them together again.

1. Demonstrate removing a puzzle piece.
2. Help the child explore the shape.
3. See what the child can do with the shape.
4. Allow him to try on his own. Give him whatever help is needed to make him feel successful.

Observing Progress:

Was the child able to work without getting frustrated?

Did the child need assistance?

Did he work alone?

Did he work with another child?

Follow-up: As the child gains in experience and efficiency, gradually move from whole object puzzles to divided object puzzles. Allowing the child to choose his own usually increases his enjoyment of the task.

chapter 6

Sociodramatic Play Activities

Sociodramatic play activities include the types of play where a child takes on roles (pretends he is someone else) and interacts with other children to carry out a pretend story. This kind of play helps children to understand themselves, their feelings, and the people around them. Social growth is probably the most obvious benefit of sociodramatic play. Through sociodramatic play, the egocentric young child begins to share fantasies and experiences with others and begins to take into account other points of view. Sociodramatic play also encourages the young child to begin to understand the roles of persons in the larger society, such as grocers, waiters and community helpers—an understanding often taken for granted by older children and adults, but requires much practice by a child in his preschool years. Sociodramatic play also promotes intellectual growth by providing opportunities for representational thinking (the idea that one thing can stand for or represent something else). It is this type of thinking that prepares the child for later school skills, such as understanding that written words can represent objects in the real world.

prop box

Goals: Helping child to:

1. Have experiences to develop ideas and thoughts
2. Come to understand his world and people in it
3. Develop creative expression

Objectives: Child will, by pantomime, role play, or puppetry:

1. Use materials in prop box as an aid to dramatic play
2. Direct the activity himself

Materials: Blocks, dolls, accessories, dress-up clothing (hats, gloves, adult shoes, pocketbooks, ties), toy phones, cash register, hats which represent occupations (firefighter, painter, conductor, nurse)

Procedure:

1. Have previously provided many interesting experiences, such as field trips, contacts with various people, recordings, books, pictures and films.
2. Provide materials as listed above.
3. Provide space and time for child-directed activity.
4. Help child who does not readily participate enter the group by suggesting some role the child can assume.

Observing Progress: Does child perform:

- Symbolic play in microsphere?
- Symbolic play in macrosphere?
- Sociodramatic play?

puppet dramatization

Goals: Helping child to:

1. Develop language skills as he speaks, listens and communicates

2. Enjoy and appreciate good literature

Objective: After becoming familiar with appropriate puppets and "May I Bring a Friend" by de Regniers, child will create dialogue and actions for puppets

Materials: Puppets

Procedure:

1. Read poem to children.

2. Allow children to choose puppets from a display on table.

3. Encourage the child to enact the story singly or in groups of two.

Observing Progress: Was each child able to speak through a puppet?

Follow-up: *Poems to Read to the Very Young,* by Josette Frank, has a collection of suitable poems (see Bibliography). Allow children to act out or pantomime their favorite poems.

poetry pantomimes

KEY SP / SM

Goals: Helping child to:

1. Appreciate poetry or verse
2. Express freedom of movement in character role
3. Share ideas by both verbal expression and body movement

Objective: In response to poetry or verse, the child will play the role of a character through pantomime.

Materials: Nursery rhymes, Mother Goose, short, action poems with limited number of characters

Procedure:

1. Read aloud the selection (example, "Little Miss Muffet").

2. Suggest the following:

   - *Pretend you are sitting on a stool eating your food.*

   - *Now pretend there's a large, dark spider hanging near your nose.*

3. Encourage discussion and creative thinking by asking questions, such as: "What else could Miss Muffet have done?" "What happened to her food?"

Observing Progress: Was the child able to respond on a symbolic play level? On a sociodramatic play level?

Follow-up: Allow child to pantomime rhymes, such as "Little Jack Horner" while others guess what the rhyme is.

parade

KEY SM SP

Goals: Helping child to:

1. Enjoy and appreciate music
2. Role play the part of a marcher
3. Express freedom of movement

Objective: To clap, step and march to music using instruments and/or costumes

Materials: A variety of instruments—purchased or homemade, a marching record, record player (or play a march on the piano), hats or costumes, if desired

Procedure:

1. Talk about parades. What is a good parade? Have you ever seen a parade? Do you like parades?
2. Have children listen to march music; listen for the beat.
3. March in place; clap hands.
4. Select an instrument; march with the music.
5. Choose a hat or costume.
6. Have a parade. March (in costume) with instruments to the time of the music.

Observing Progress: Did the child move freely to the music? Could he perform in "parade style"?

Follow-up:

- Make up a marching chant and march to it. Your chant could go something like this:

  Left, right, left, right,
  March along, sing a song.

  Left, right, left, right,
  Why don't you come along?

- Play "Follow the Leader".

131

a grandparent's visit

KEY: SM SP

Goals: Helping child to:

1. Role play family members
2. Increase language usage
3. Move through sensorimotor play to symbolic and/or sociodramatic play

Objective: To role play a grandparent coming to visit

Materials: Grandmother or Grandfather outfit from the dress-up corner, large pocketbook or suitcase, and surprises (almost anything): buttons, toys, beads, pens, crayons, small books, and so on.

Procedure:

1. The grandparent (the child) comes to visit bringing a suitcase containing surprises which she or he can give to each child.

2. The "grandparent" describes each object he is giving out.

Observing Progress: Was the child able to role play the grandparent? Did he verbalize about the objects as he passed them out to his "grandchildren"?

Follow-up: Two or three children role play going to the grandparents' house for a visit.

moving day

Goals: Helping child to:

1. Develop gross and fine motor skills
2. Role play given character
3. Move through sensorimotor play to symbolic play and sociodramatic play

Objective: To role play a "furniture mover"

Materials: A dollhouse (homemade or commercial), doll furniture (improvised from cardboard boxes or purchased), a large play truck or pasteboard box, and dollhouse dolls.

Procedure:

1. Place an empty dollhouse and a large truck or boxful of dollhouse furniture in a section of the room.
2. Tell the children a new family has must moved into the neighborhood and they need to move all their furniture into the dollhouse.

3. Have the children take the items off the truck and move them into the house.

Observing Progress: Could the child role play the "furniture mover"? Did the child engage in dramatic play in the following ways:

- Imitative role play?
- Make-believe with objects?
- Persist in sociodramatic for five minutes or more?

- Interact with peers?
- Use language to maintain play?

Follow-up: Allow children to move actual furnishings in the room (if light enough to lift). Let them rearrange or design, but they should be expected to put everything back in place.

restaurant

Goals: Helping child to:
1. Increase language skills
2. Engage in role play
3. Move into sociodramatic play

Objective: To role play a restaurant worker or a family member eating in a restaurant

Materials: Children's tables, chairs, play dishes, silverware, and cooking pans, paper cups for serving water, food, and (optional) chef's hat, aprons, play money

Procedure:
1. Set up one of the children's tables as a counter with chairs on one side. Waitresses and waiters wear aprons and the chef wears a hat made out of a piece of old sheet with elastic around the bottom. There could also be a dishwasher and a cashier with a "money" box complete with play coins or buttons.

2. Provide the restaurant with dry cereals, raisins, nutritious snack foods, or something the children have cooked the day before.

3. Let the children enact various scenes associated with going to a restaurant. Some possibilities:
   - Dressing up in clothes to "go out to dinner" (perhaps even calling a babysitter).
   - Making parking spaces outside the restaurant (with masking tape) for cars.
   - Setting tables.
   - Waiting on customers.

   Those children not willing to engage in dramatic play but wanting to join in the activity, could make colored place mats for use in the restaurant.

Observing Progress: Did the child engage in dramatic play?

Follow-up: Plan a "birthday party" for an imaginary friend. You could have music, dancing, pretend birthday cake with candles, and pretend presents to open. Don't forget to clean up!

grocery store

Goals: Helping child to:

1. Develop concepts of stores, money, and foods
2. Develop language skills
3. Move through sensorimotor play into symbolic and sociodramatic play

Objective: To role play grocer and/or shopper

Materials: Tables, cupboards or boxes, empty cans and food cartons, imitation or real fruits and vegetables, cash register with colored chips for toy money, baskets or bags to put "groceries" in, aprons for the clerks, self-adhesive colored dots or tape to price food

Procedure: Give each carton or can a certain number of dots. For example: soup, two dots; milk, three dots; eggs, four dots, and so on. The dots represent the price, and each child "pays" with corresponding colored chips or discs.

You can direct a child to go to the store for "a can of soup" or to be a homemaker shopping for food. You can go to the store and ask the "clerk" for directions to where certain food items can be found.

Continue play as long as interest remains and time allows. You should participate but remain unintrusive.

Observing Progress: Was the child successful in role play?

(Keep a record of the various types and dates of child's sociodramatic play.)

Follow-up: Have materials readily available in the doll corner for children to initiate this activity on their own.

whisper tube talking

KEY: SM

Goals: Helping child to:

1. Increase language usage
2. Develop concepts of loud and soft
3. Increase auditory discrimination skills
4. Interact with peers

Objective: To whisper to one child something which has been whispered by another

Materials: Tubes from tissue paper or paper towels

Procedures:

1. The children sit in a circle, each with a paper tube.
2. You think of a sentence and whisper it through your tube to the child beside you in the circle.
3. Each child whispers what he heard to to the next child.

4. The last child says the sentence out loud and then you say your sentence. If the sentences match, the children have done a good job of tube talking.

You should choose sentences of immediate interest to the children. "We're going to have ice cream today." Or "Tomorrow is Marcia's birthday."

Sentences can get more complicated and difficult as the children become adept. Soon children will be able to initiate the game and play by themselves.

Encourage children to speak softly or whisper to avoid hurting ears. It is good to start with just two or three children and very simple sentences. You may find that a shy child will whisper through the tube when he will not speak aloud.

Observing Progress: Were all children able to participate?

Were they all able to maintain a whisper while using the tube?

Follow-up: Dramatize the *Quiet, Noisy Book*, by Margaret Wise Brown (see Bibliography).

telephone talking

Goals: Helping child to:

1. Increase language usage
2. Interact with peers
3. Develop auditory discrimination
4. Engage in symbolic play and/or sociodramatic play

Objective: To act out talking on the telephone

Materials: Toy telephone (or real phones which sometimes can be obtained from the local telephone exchange)

Procedure: Very little direction is needed for children to engage in telephone play. If direction is needed, you might try the following:

1. Have child call to ask another to come play.
2. Have child call home to talk to mommy or daddy.
3. Allow children to assume adult roles and call each other for reasons pertaining to the role, such as a parent with a sick child who must call a doctor.
4. If the child does not want to make a call, allow him to receive one. It is sometimes easier to respond to questions rather than ask them. Encourage the child to say hello and goodbye.

Observing Progress: Did the child engage in symbolic play? Sociodramatic play?

Follow-up: Allow the child to call home—really dial his own number and talk with someone at home. Have someone home prepared to take his call.

a story of my own

KEY: SM SP

Goals: Helping child to:
1. Verbalize from own experience
2. Engage in storytelling

Objective: Prompted by flannelboard and visual aids, child tells a story of his own creation

Materials: Flannelboard; miscellaneous, visual aids; a story known to the children, such as *Millions of Cats*, "Three Billy Goats Gruff" or "Goldilocks" (see Bibliography)

Procedure:
1. One child begins story using whatever visual aids he desires, another child continues, and so on until all children have participated.
2. Do not be concerned if story leaves the usual story line. The development of the child's imagination and his creativity are what you are after here.

Observing Progress: Were the children able to respond verbally to stimulus of visual aids and other peers?

Follow-up: Tape record the storytelling. Then play back the tape, using the flannelboard and aids. Let the children listen and each identify his or her voice.

acting out stories

Goals: Helping child to:
1. Develop large motor skills
2. Foster creativity
3. Increase language usage
4. Increase symbolic play and sociodramatic play

Objectives:
1. To act out a dramatic element
2. To dramatize (pantomime) a story

Materials: None or props as desired

Procedures:

1. It is best to start creative dramatics very spontaneously and informally, either by introducing a dramatic element as the children are moving to music or by seizing upon some moment in ongoing play to illustrate that children look like something other than themselves.

   You could say, "Hey, that music sounds like popcorn popping. Can anyone dance like a popcorn kernel?"

2. After informal attempts, such as the one suggested above, go on to simple dramatics. Relate to some project or story with which the children are familiar.

   I wonder if you could be a seed—growing in the dark, coming up through the ground, feeling the sun's warmth, and turning into a plant.

3. Once children can accept pretending to be something further from their own lives than daddies, mommies or firefighters, you might suggest that they act out a whole story. At first it might be easier for you to read the story while selected children pantomime it. Use a variety of short pantomimes as the opportunities arise.

Observing Progress:

Was the child able to accept pretending to be something removed from his immediate life?

Is he ready to verbalize a well-known story?

Follow-up:

Use a well-known story with simple and repetitious text, such as "Caps for Sale", "Three Billy Goats Gruff", or "Goldilocks". (See Bibliography.) Have children pantomime story, then perform again, adding words in their own language.

BIBLIOGRAPHY

Ackerman, Jeanne V. *Play the Perceptual Motor Way.* Bernie Straub Publishing Co., Inc. and Special Child Publications, Seattle, WA, 1975.

Baker, Katherine Read. *Let's Play Outdoors.* National Association for Education of Young Children, NY, 1966.

Buttler, Annie L., Gotts, Edward E., Quisenberry, Nancy L. *Play As Development.* Charles E. Merrill Publishing Co., Columbus, O, 1978.

Garvey, Catherine. *Play.* Harvard University Press, Cambridge, MA, 1977.

Herron, R.E. and Sutton-Smith, Brian (eds.). *Child's Play.* John Wiley and Sons, Inc., NY, 1971.

Hodgden, Laurel et al. *School Before Six: A Diagnostic Approach.* Volume II. CEMREL, Inc., St. Louis, MO, 1974.

Leeper, Sarah H., Skipper, Dora S. and Witherspoon, Ralph L. *Good Schools for Young Children.* Macmillan Publishing Co., Inc., NY, 1979.

Markus, Patricia Maloney. *Play: Children's Business.* Association for Childhood Education, Intl., Washington, DC, 1974.

Marzollo, Jean and Lloyd, Janice. *Learning Through Play.* Harper and Row, NY, 1972.

Montessori, Marie. *The Discovery of the Child.* Fides Publishers, Inc., Notre Dame, IN, 1967.

Newbury, Josephine. *More Kindergarten Resources.* John Knox Press, Atlanta, GA, 1974.

Oetting, Phyllis B. *Everybody Wins.* Academic Therapy Publication, San Rafael, CA, 1974.

Orem, R.C. ed. *A Montessori Handbook.* G.P. Putnam Sons, NY, 1965.

Piaget, Jean. *Play Dreams and Imitation in Childhood.* W.W. Norton & Co., Inc., NY, 1962.

Pitcher, Evelyn Goodenaugh, Lasher, Miriam G., Feinburg. Sylvia G. and Braun, Linda Abrams. *Helping Young Children Learn,* 2nd edition. Charles E. Merrill Publishing Co., Columbus, O, 1974.

Taylor, Barbara J. *A Child Goes Forth.* Brigham Young University Press, Provo, UT, 1972.

Taylor, Barbara J. *When I Do, I Learn.* Brigham Young University Press, Provo, UT, 1974.

Watrin, Rita and Furfey, Paul Hanley. *Learning Activities for the Young Preschool Child.* D. Van Nostrand Co., NY, 1978.

Weikert, Daivid P., Rogers, Linda, Adcock, Carolyn and McClelland, Donna. *The Cognitively Oriented Curriculum.* ERIC-NAEYC, Urbana, IL, 1977.

Wolfgang, Charles H. *Helping Aggressive and Passive Preschoolers Through Play.* Charles E. Merrill Publishing Co., Columbus, O, 1977.

BOOKS AND RECORDS FOR USE WITH CHILDREN

Caps for Sale, by Esphyr Slobodkins, Addison Wesley, 1947.

Count and See, by Taner Hoban, Macmillan, 1972.

Golden Song Book, by Katharine T. Wessells, Golden Press (Western Publishing), 1964.

Hole is to Dig, A First Book of First Definitions, by Ruth Krauss, Harper & Row, 1952.

Little Blue & Little Yellow, by Leo Leonni. Astor-Honor, 1959.

Little Engine that Could, by Watty Piper. Platt, 1976.

The Little House, by Virginia Lee Burton. Houghton-Mifflin, 1978.

May I Bring a Friend?, by Beatrice S. Regniers. Atheneium, 1964.

Millions of Cats, by Nanda Gag. Coward, 1977.

Mod Marchers (Record), by Hap Palmer, Educational Activities, Inc., Freeport, NY 11520.

Music for Early Childhood (Record), Choate, R.A., et al. American Book Co., New York, NY., 1970.

Numbers of Things, by Helen Oxenbury. Watts, 1968.

Poems to Read to the Very Young, by Josette Frank. Random, 1961.

Quiet, Noisy Book, by Margaret Wise Brown. Harper & Row, 1950.

The Snowy Day, by Ezra Jack Keats. Viking Press, 1964.

Stone Soup, by Marcia Brown. Scribner, 1947.

Wake Up City, by A. Tressault. Lothrop, Lee and Shepherd, 1957.

INDEX

APPENDIX

Stamp Pad for pages 54, 55

Fit small aluminum frozen food containers with thin pieces of cellulose sponge which have been cut to fit the bottom of the pan. Saturate the sponge with tempera paint which has been mixed somewhat thicker than the directions call for. Add paint to the pad as needed. After use, wash pads and dry out.

Homemade Play Dough for pages 66, 72, 74, 75

1 cup flour, 1 cup salt, ½ cup water
(1 tablespoon salad oil will keep mixture pliable)
Mix and knead thoroughly. Add food coloring as desired.

Shapes Card for page 109

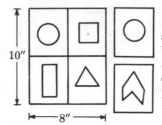

Make a card (8″ x 10″). Divide into quarters. In one quarter, draw a circle; the other, a square; the third, a rectangle; the fourth, a triangle (see illustration).

On a set of smaller paper cards (each the size of one quarter of the board), draw one shape. On some cards, draw shapes *not* shown on the large card. Make 26-52 cards.

About the Authors

Dr. Charles H. Wolfgang holds a Master of Education degree in Higher Education from the University of Southern California and a Doctor of Philosophy degree from the University of Pittsburgh. He is currently Associate Professor of Early and Middle Childhood Education at the Ohio State University. He is the author of *Helping Aggressive and Passive Preschoolers Through Play* (Charles E. Merrill, 1977) and *Solving Discipline Problems: Strategies for Classroom Teachers* (Allyn and Bacon, 1980). Dr. Wolfgang is a popular speaker and an active participant in the Association for the Education of Young Children.

Dr. Mary E. Wolfgang holds a Master of Science from the University of Pittsburgh in Child Development and a Doctor of Philosophy from the Ohio State University. Her recent article on "Family Stress and Child Abuse" can be found in *Stress* (1981), published by the Association for Childhood Education International. She is married to Charles Wolfgang and they have one child.

Bea Mackender has taught in elementary school for seven years and is the author of *Instructional Objectives: Title I and DPPF Programs*, published by the Department of Special Program Development, Columbus Public Schools, Columbus, Ohio. She is the mother of two children, ages 7 and 5, and holds a Bachelor of Science in Education degree from the Ohio State University.